Baby Boomer Retirement Roadmap

FIVE KEYS TO ENJOYING THE LIFESTYLE YOU WANT FOR THE REST OF YOUR LIFE

By Denny Frasiolas
and Artie Bernaducci

Copyright © 2020 Denny Frasiolas and Artie Bernaducci
All rights reserved.

Advisory services are offered through Retirement Income Advisory Group LLC, a Registered Investment Advisor in the state of New Jersey. Insurance products and services are offered through All Access Brokerage, LLC, an affiliated company. Retirement Income Advisory Group LLC and All Access Brokerage, LLC are not affiliated with or endorsed by the Social Security Administration or any government agency.

The contents of this book are provided for informational purposes only and are not intended to serve as the basis for any financial decisions. Any tax, legal, or estate planning information is general in nature. It should not be construed as legal or tax advice. Always consult an attorney or tax professional regarding the applicability of this information to your unique situation.

Information presented is believed to be factual and up-to-date, but we do not guarantee its accuracy, and it should not be regarded as a complete analysis of the subjects discussed. All expressions of opinion are those of the author as of the date of publication and are subject to change. Content should not be construed as personalized investment advice, nor should it be interpreted as an offer to buy or sell any securities mentioned. A financial advisor should be consulted before implementing any of the strategies presented.

Investing involves risk, including the potential loss of principal. No investment strategy can guarantee a profit or protect against loss in periods of declining values. Any references to protection benefits or guaranteed/lifetime income streams refer only to fixed insurance products, not securities or investment products. Insurance and annuity product guarantees are backed by the financial strength and claims-paying ability of the issuing insurance company.

This publication is licensed to the individual reader only. Duplication or distribution by any means, including email, disk, photocopy, and recording, to a person other than the original purchaser, is a violation of international copyright law.

Publisher:

**Retirement Income Advisory Group, LLC,
1460 Route 9 N, Suite 210 A,
Woodbridge, NJ 07095**
www.Retire-USA.com

Baby Boomer Retirement Roadmap
by Denny Frasiolas and Artie Bernaducci

ISBN: 9798643355861

While they have made every effort to verify the information provided in this publication, neither the authors nor the publisher assumes any responsibility for errors in, omissions from, or different interpretations of the subject matter.

The information herein may be subject to varying laws and practices in different areas, states, and countries. The reader assumes all responsibility for use of the information.

Table of Contents

This Book Is for You If i
Baby Boomer Retirement Roadmap: Five Keys to Enjoying the Lifestyle You Want for the Rest of Your Life iii
   Making a Plan v
   Planning for the Retirement Mountain vi
   Becoming Retirement Ready vii
Key #1: Understanding the Baby Boomer Retirement Challenge 1
   Why Planning for Retirement Is Harder Now Than Before 3
   Keys to Taking Retirement Planning Seriously 9
   What to Do When It Seems Too Late to Plan 12
   Key Factors in Retirement Planning 13
Key #2: Navigating Comfortably Up and Down the Retirement Mountain 17
   The Retirement Mountain: Two Phases of Planning 19
   Retirement Income Stool: The Three Legs 21
   Factors That Influence Your Retirement Lifestyle 22
   The Difference Between Accumulation and Distribution. 26
   Accumulation Phase: Keys to Maximization 30
   Distribution Phase: Keys to Maximization 46
   Case Study: Mia and Walt 55
   What We've Learned in This Chapter 56
   Checklist: Navigating the Retirement Mountain 56
Key #3: Ways to Help You Achieve the Best Social Security Benefits Possible 59
   The History of Social Security 61

    The Building Blocks of Social Security 64

    Social Security Choices 68

    The Retirement Decision 70

    Spousal Benefits 73

    Children's Benefits... 75

    Taxation of Social Security 76

    How Divorce Affects Social Security 78

    Starting Again If You Make the Wrong Choice 79

    Getting Advice... 80

    Recent Claiming Changes... 80

    What We've Learned in This Chapter........................... 81

    Checklist: Choosing the Right Social Security Filing Option 81

Key #4: Protecting Your Health and Financial Security for Life 83

    Key Factors Influencing the Protection of Your Financial Security.. 84

    The Ongoing Need for Life Insurance......................... 86

    Health Insurance in Retirement and Medicare 88

    Long-Term Care Insurance 92

    Case Study: Grace 94

    What We've Learned in This Chapter........................... 95

    Checklist: Protecting Your Health and Financial Security 96

Key #5: Passing Wealth on to the Next Generation 97

    Key Factors Influencing Your Estate Planning............. 98

    Steps for Creating an Estate Plan 100

    Passing Assets on to Family During Lifetime...............101

    The Role of Life Insurance in Estate Planning.............101

What Happens If You Are Unable to Make Decisions in Later Life? 105

Case Study: Miriam 105

What We've Learned in This Chapter.......................................106

Checklist: Passing Wealth on to the Next Generation 107

Appendices 109

Appendix 1: Nine Retirement Mistakes to Avoid 111

Appendix 2: Milestones for the Retirement Lifestyle You Want 117

Retirement Ready Milestone #1: Knowing Your Current Net Worth..118

Retirement Ready Milestone #2: Knowing Where Your Money Goes Now 122

Retirement Ready Milestone #3: Envisioning Your Retirement 123

Retirement Ready Milestone #4: Knowing What You'll Need in Retirement 124

Checklist: Achieving the Retirement Lifestyle You Want 125

Appendix 3: The ABCD of Medicare and How to Avoid the Five Most Common Enrollment Mistakes...127

Where to Go for Help . . . Is There Anybody Out There?...128

Simple Explanations of the Four Parts of Medicare:..........129

Four Enrollment Periods 131

Watch Your Step! The Five Most Common Medicare Enrollment Mistakes We See Happen Explained 134

Appendix 4: What Every Pre- and Post- Retiree Needs to Know About the Recent Social Security Claiming Changes and What They Mean for You! 139

What Has Changed?..139

Deemed Filing 140

File and Suspend..141

Restricted Application 142
Where Do We Go From Here? 144
What You Need to Know About the New Tax Law 147
Your Next Steps: What Do You Do Now? 149
If You Prefer, Do It Yourself 151
About Retirement Income Advisory Group 153
Our Mission 153
About Denny Frasiolas 155
About Artie Bernaducci 157
Acknowledgments 159

This Book Is for You If . . .

You should take time to study and consider this book if one or more of the following applies to you:

• You are a baby boomer, meaning you were born between 1946 to 1964.

• You've experienced a major life change recently, such as moving to a new home, changing jobs, retiring, receiving an inheritance, facing a divorce, selling your home, etc.

• You are thinking about your retirement and want to ensure you have taken all the right steps to make it as enjoyable and stress-free as possible.

• You have been wondering about whether you need financial advice, but you're just not sure of the best way to go about getting it.

• You worry about the unpredictable economy and wonder what effect it will have on your long-term finances.

• You are interested in legal, ethical, and effective strategies to help you pay less in taxes—both now and in retirement.

• You have heard some people say the government cannot afford to continue the current Social Security arrangements forever, and you are concerned about what this means for you.

• You are worried about the volatility and risks of the stock market.

• You worked hard for the money you have earned and saved, and you want to ensure you pass something on to your kids and grandkids without the government getting its hands on too much of it.

• You already have some savings and retirement plans but are not sure if they are enough to last for as long as you may need them.

• You know you need to invest your money wisely for the future but are confused by the whole range of options available.

• You realize you may live a long time after retirement and are worried about what will happen if you become weak or frail or even need long-term care services.

• You are concerned about what will happen to your spouse if they are left alone in their senior years.

• You already retired and are dissatisfied with the income produced by your assets and investments.

• You want to make sure you and your dependents get their fair share of Social Security money after years of paying into it.

BABY BOOMER RETIREMENT ROADMAP

Five Keys to Enjoying the Lifestyle You Want for the Rest of Your Life

Today, millions of Americans in the "baby boomer" generation approach retirement with more opportunities and more challenges than any previous generation.

Our parents and grandparents often retired after long periods of employment with a single employer or having made very few job changes during their lives.

When they retired, they could often rely on a Social Security benefit backed up by a healthy pension from their long-term employer.

Typically, they would live only a few years after retirement, and usually they would be able to do this without major financial worries.

Even if they didn't quite live a luxurious lifestyle, they could often expect to be comfortable for the remainder of their golden years.

Today, however, we face a very different set of circumstances. The way we live, work, and plan our finances has changed—in some cases, significantly.

Now:

- We live longer.
- We enjoy a more active lifestyle in retirement.
- We expect to maintain high standards of living in retirement.

These are largely improvements as far as our life and lifestyle prospects. However, there are also some substantial tradeoffs, such as:

- Traditional pensions are disappearing.
- Market and economic booms and busts have left people concerned and confused about investing their hard-earned money.
- Health care costs are rising.
- Life is unpredictable, and we never know when we might need access to our money.
- Social Security faces enormous pressure as the number of people in retirement increases, and the increasing costs are shared amongst fewer people in the workforce. (This has already led to new legislation affecting Social Security benefits.)
- The range of investment options is complex, making it hard to know who to trust. (Even television personalities have now become financial "gurus.")

The result is we need to be more careful than ever before about making our money last.

So, perhaps it's not surprising many Americans these days find their retirement plans coming up short. It's now a real concern that many retirees today could outlive their financial assets if they attempt to maintain their preretirement standards of living.

The good news is there is something you can do about it.

Making a Plan

It couldn't be clearer that, whatever your current situation, now is the time to stop and check how effective your current strategy is for building a retirement nest egg and ensuring it will last the rest of your life.

> **Many retirees today could outlive their financial assets if they attempt to maintain their preretirement standards of living.**

Don't have a retirement strategy?

Well, bear this in mind . . .

Wells Fargo reports those with a planning mindset (people who set concrete financial goals) accumulated three times more in retirement assets versus those without one.[1]

Fortunately, it's never too late—or too early—to work on the right strategy.

And it's better to work on it with the right information and support.

Here's the key . . .

Regardless of how you envision your retirement, these days, you are primarily responsible for planning how to get there.

Let us make one thing clear (we'll come back to it later on in the book):

> *Having a 401(k), IRA, or another arrangement in place does not mean you have a complete plan for retirement.*

---

[1] Wells Fargo. 2018. "2018 Wells Fargo Retirement Study." https://www08.wellsfargomedia.com/assets/pdf/commercial/retirement-employee-benefits/perspectives/2018_Wells_Fargo_Retirement_Survey_WP.pdf

A few additional steps are necessary.

First, you have to make the best choices for building your nest egg. Then you have to decide how best to manage and protect the nest egg you've worked so hard to build. You will also need to ensure your nest egg generates a strong enough income stream to last you a lifetime and remain large enough to provide the lifestyle you want.

Planning for the Retirement Mountain

Here's another important concept we will return to later in the book.

Planning for retirement is like climbing a mountain—*and* coming back down.

With this in mind, you need one approach for climbing the mountain and another for coming down the other side safely and comfortably.

When you're taking a challenging path in any area of your life, you probably want to do it with an experienced guide, similar to Sherpas who accompany mountaineers in the Himalayas.

That way, you can be more confident in your plans for the ascent and descent.

It's the same idea when it comes to the different phases of your retirement planning.

Many people feel they need the assurance of a guide to help them work out what they need to do and when they need to do it.

> **When you're taking a challenging path in any area of your life, you probably want to do it with an experienced guide.**

We like to think of ourselves as resembling the Sherpas. We use our extensive experiences in the complex terrain of financial planning to help our clients feel more protected and comfortable.

The challenge for many people is the process of planning for retirement requires so many decisions, and your priorities usually change depending on where you are in your life. What is most important for you when you are twenty is often not your main priority when you are forty, and something that may be crucial at age forty may not even be on your list of priorities at all by the time you are sixty.

By helping people make decisions, we act as the Sherpas for our clients as they plan to traverse what we call the "retirement mountain."

But we have found many people beyond those we serve as our clients need support in their retirement preparations. So, while we can't be personal guides for everyone, we can set out a roadmap highlighting what we believe is most important for the climb.

That's our aim in writing this book.

Becoming Retirement Ready

Do you need a guide to help ensure you're retirement ready?

You might if you are between fifty and seventy-five years of age—whether you are retired or very close to it. We'd like to help you in your goal of becoming retirement ready.

There are a number of benefits associated with being truly retirement ready.

For instance, when you are retirement ready, you can be more confident that you will have the income you want in retirement and that you'll continue to enjoy the lifestyle you want for the rest of your life. Some of the other key benefits include the following:

- If you are heading toward retirement, you are still climbing the retirement mountain, and you'll discover ways to help maximize your retirement readiness for both the peak and descent.
- If you are already retired, you're already making your way down the retirement mountain, and you'll discover ways to help ensure the nest egg you've worked so hard to accumulate provides the most income possible for the rest of your life.

We aim to make this book as helpful as possible without filling it with jargon, unlike many other retirement books available on the market today.

We've answered many of the questions we are most typically asked, and we've provided a roadmap here in this book to help you through the following five stages of:

1. Understanding the Baby Boomer Retirement Challenge
2. Navigating Comfortably Up and Down the Retirement Mountain
3. Selecting the Right Social Security Payout
4. Protecting Your Health and Financial Comfort for Life
5. Passing Wealth on to the Next Generation

It's your retirement, and you've worked hard for it! Our roadmap is designed to help you live the lifestyle you want for the rest of your life. If you're ready to get started, let's dive in!

KEY #1:

Understanding the Baby Boomer Retirement Challenge

"You're called 'boomers' because 'boom' is the sound most of you will make when you crash into your retirement years."

The first big challenge most people face when they think about retirement is they don't really have a clear plan for it.

When preparing for retirement, people often assume they have some pensions in place and some investments that can get them through the remainder of their lifetime. But, most of the time, they haven't sat down and really worked out the necessary details.

Sometimes that's because retirement still seems a long way off. In other cases, it's because the whole thing seems so confusing or overwhelming to the point that they think, "out of sight, out of mind." Regardless, they may end up procrastinating until it's too late—which can end up costing them big time!

Often, they don't understand planning for retirement really isn't all that hard—especially when you work with an experienced guide. The process can also be made much easier when you break it down into more "bite-sized" steps.

One of the most important steps is to start actually planning for your retirement and understanding the importance of that planning.

In this first step of the retirement planning roadmap, we want to help you get this foundation right because everything else will be built upon it. And we all know, the stronger the foundation is, the stronger the structure built on top of it will be.

By the end of this chapter, we hope you'll have a firm foundation and a good understanding in place for moving on to the next step.

In this section, we will look at:

- Why Planning for Retirement Is Harder Now Than Before
- Keys to Taking Retirement Planning Seriously
- What to Do When It Seems Too Late to Plan
- Key Factors in Retirement Planning

Why Planning for Retirement Is Harder Now Than Before

Before mobile phones, the internet, and complex financial products, life used to be less complicated in many ways.

While we may be nostalgic for certain aspects, it certainly doesn't mean life was better back in the day—there are certainly aspects of modern life that we wouldn't want to trade. Yet, there are several reasons planning for our retirement years is now much more complicated than it used to be.

> I think the Baby Boom has enjoyed itself, maybe sometimes a little too much, and we're continuing to enjoy ourselves, maybe a little too much.
>
> P J O'Rourke, Writer.

Among the most notable reasons for this are:

- Changing demographics
- Different employment patterns
- Longer life spans
- Uncertain Social Security
- A wider range of ways to plan for the future (which, in turn, can lead to confusion and overwhelming feelings about what to do)

Let's take a closer look at each of these elements.

• Changing demographics

People around retirement age now generally originate from what is known as the "baby boomer" generation.

The "baby boomer" name arose from the unusual spike in the birth rates after the Second World War. Young men and women who had been unable to settle down and raise families through the war years suddenly entered a period of peace and prosperity and got to work making up for lost time.

Generally, anyone born between 1946 and 1964 is considered a "baby boomer," so it follows many people retiring now—or thinking about retirement—are part of this generation.

In general, despite some economic storms along the way, our baby boomer generation has probably enjoyed a higher standard of living than our parents and grandparents did.

According to Forrester Research, older shoppers now not only make up a larger segment of the population than ever, but they also are the biggest spenders because of the extra cash built up over the years.

For example, in 1973, older consumers accounted for 25 percent of discretionary spending, but this grew to 35 percent by 2013.[2]

One of the challenges we face now in looking ahead to retirement is some from this era have overenjoyed the good times and didn't prepare for a rainy day.

Some have borrowed rather than saved, and they have little in the way of savings for the future.

This issue is compounded by the fact that this generation did not follow the example of their parents by having large numbers of children.

At a very localized level, one couple needs to have two children to "replace" themselves. In fact, on average, they need slightly more than two, allowing for those who sadly pass away young.

---

[2] Ashley Lutz. *Business Insider.* June 2, 2015. "Baby Boomers are the sexiest consumers in retail." https://www.businessinsider.com/baby-boomers-spend-the-most-money-2015-6

The reality in the U.S. now, however, is the average fertility rate—the number of children born per adult—is much fewer than this. It's closer to 1.5.[3]

This means, for every six baby boomers, only about four people have been born in the next generation.

This is what we mean by an "aging population." There are fewer young people (i.e., people in the workforce and lined up ready to come into the workforce) than there are in the older generations who are nearing the end of their working years.

In theory, this means those four children have to work harder to support the six from the older generation when they can no longer work.

In practice, even if they were willing to do this—an unlikely scenario, given they will also have to work harder to support their own finances—the current system of pensions may well be unsustainable for some of the other reasons we discuss.

• Different employment patterns

There are also different employment patterns today than there were in the past.

In our parents' generation, many people spent their entire lives working for one corporation, and many of these offered pension plans with retirement income benefits linked to what people earned while working.

At the time, the easy advice was to get a good job at a good company, work hard, and then end up with a nice pension.

---

[3] Julia Belluz. Vox. May 15, 2019. "The historically low birthrate, explained in 3 charts."
https://www.vox.com/science-and-health/2018/5/22/17376536/fertility-rate-united-states-births-women

However, the key problem here is the same demographic change we mentioned above.

Many of these big company pension schemes started in the fifties and the sixties when there were around ten to eleven workers for every pension recipient. At that time, the economics looked good.

> **In many pension schemes, there are more pensioners than workers.**

Over time, though, the situation has actually reversed in many cases, and there are now often more pensioners than workers in these plans.

Although many of these pension funds built up substantial assets, the financial demands, combined with the changing demographics, mean they cannot always be sustained.

With companies no longer offering competitive pensions, many workers no longer feel compelled to stay with one company, leading to more turnover in the workforce. The days of retiring after a lifetime at one company are dwindling. This in turn can disincentivize companies from offering pensions, as some boards figure it's not worth investing in the professional development of workers who may leave after a few years.

In addition to this, the remaining pensions' benefits need to be paid out for a longer period of time due to increased American longevity. This leads to our next component.

- **Longer life spans**

In the early days of pension plans, many people did not live long beyond retirement—often just two or three years on average.

Nowadays, many people can expect to live fifteen to twenty years (or more) after retirement —often in good health.

That's time that has to be paid for by these pension benefits, and, often, people hope to enjoy the same standard of living they enjoyed while they were working. Now they just have more time to spend money!

• Uncertain Social Security

The story of Social Security is similar to the history we just covered of company pensions.

Social Security was initially set up to prevent the elderly from having to live an undignified life in poverty when they were not able to work anymore. But this program was never meant to provide one's primary retirement income benefits.

Social Security works on a pay-as-you-go principle, meaning the contributions of current workers are used to pay the income benefits of retired people.

Unlike a lot of company pension funds, the money to fund Social Security benefits has not been set aside in advance.

> **There is a kind of fear, approaching a panic, that's spreading through the baby boom generation, which has suddenly discovered that it will have to provide for its own retirement.**
>
> **Ron Chernow, Writer.**

This approach worked in the days when the population was growing and the active members paying into Social Security outnumbered those withdrawing from it.

For example, three or four active workers might be paying into the system for every retired person receiving benefits.

This was possible because the population steadily grew.

As we explained prior, though, the roles are now becoming reversed due to the shrinking numbers of active workers. In order to sustain the Social Security system over the long term, we will need to make some changes. Some of the changes on the table mean choosing among options such as:

- Increased retirement ages
- Smaller payouts
- Increased worker contributions

In fact, we could end up with a mix of all three. But we cannot expect to rely on future generations to finance people in retirement as they have done in the past. Some would even argue the whole Social Security system is unsustainable.

As we'll explain later, Social Security remains an important part of your retirement calculations, but it is not something you want to rely solely on to sustain your desired standard of living in retirement.

• A wider range of ways to plan for the future

Today, we also have numerous financial products and services that could be used for retirement planning. While this may seem like a good thing, it can actually lead people to feel overwhelmed and, in turn, procrastinate until it is too late.

Your parents probably worked for one company for most of their lives, and they likely had a nice 401(k) or company pension to retire on at age sixty.

They may also have collected Social Security, and life was fairly good. They might have even had a few different pensions generating income for them, but, overall, the arrangements were usually straightforward.

Now, as we'll see in later chapters, a confusing array of different options to choose from—not to mention the frequency of job changes an average worker will experience—allows people to acquire many different types of investments and pensions over their working lives.

We aim to clear away some of the fog from this later in the book, but the sheer range of choices can be a factor that makes the process difficult for many people.

Keys to Taking Retirement Planning Seriously

One of the questions people most often ask when it comes to retirement finances is, "When should I start planning for my retirement?"

The obvious answer is it's never too soon to start planning for retirement.

> When you know what you want your retirement to look like, it becomes possible to work out how much it will cost.

There are several common mistakes we see people make when thinking about retirement, including:

• No Retirement Goal

Some people have no idea when they want to retire nor what they want their retirement to look like.

So, wherever you are in life right now, you should start by deciding what you want your retirement to look like. Then you can work out how much it will cost and how best to pay for it.

The good news is, this problem tends to be one of the easiest to fix. We provide some tools to help you do that at the end of this book.

• Having No Plan

Some people know they want to retire and have a retirement goal in place, but do not have a plan for how to retire.

Setting your retirement goal means deciding what you want your retirement to look like. The plan is how you actually hope to make it happen.

Without this, you may face significant challenges when retirement arrives, as many factors are out of your control.

Again, we'll show you some strategies to consider at the end of this book.

• Not Saving Enough

When you know what you want your retirement to look like and work out how much it will cost, you can then take the steps and contributions necessary to make it happen.

The reality is many people underestimate what they will need to fund the retirement they want.

There are many basic calculators available that will help you determine whether or not you're saving enough to reach your retirement goal.

• Starting Too Late

Starting too late is one of the most common problems we see, and it is the most difficult to fix. That's why you might hear the frequent statement that the most valuable retirement asset you possess is time.

We always assume it will be easier to find the money in ten years than it is today, but reality usually does not reflect this.

The truth is, you'll always have expenses and demands on your finances.

Then, what happens is, you might reach age fifty-five and wish you'd started saving back when you were thirty-five.

If you were able to create the habit of saving for retirement early, you likely have more confidence now, closer to your retirement years, that you'll have it all taken care of.

However, if you haven't planned so far ahead, the good news is it is still never too late to take action.

• Not Making the Most of Opportunities

There are many ways you can get the best out of your options for retirement planning, such as taking advantage of 401(k) matching from an employer or maximizing your tax deferral with your IRA.

You can also leverage many other opportunities to save more for retirement.

Our aim is to help you make the most of these opportunities.

• Failing to Track Results

How you save today will differ from how you save ten years from now. As you age, you'll generally want to reduce risk and invest less aggressively.

You'll also want to review your retirement savings annually to make sure you're on track to reach your goals. Setting retirement goals and tracking your progress can provide powerful motivation.

> **We always assume it will be easier to find the money in ten years than it is today, but reality usually does not reflect this.**

You might create a chart that shows you climbing closer to your goal. Or you may track your progress in a ledger or spreadsheet. In any case, you choose whatever method of tracking and measurement helps motivate you—as long as you are taking action.

In reality, you are on your own these days much more than ever before. You're entirely responsible for your retirement. It's up to you to save for your retirement—not your employer and not the government.

It's not complicated, but it does require planning and a course of action that you can and will follow through. With this book, we aim to help you develop a roadmap to do exactly that.

What to Do When It Seems Too Late to Plan

Of course, the earlier you start planning, the more time your money will have to grow, and the less it will cost you to reach your retirement goals.

Here's an example.

If you invest $5,000 a year each year until age sixty-five and assume a 7 percent return, the difference in the outcome is enormous.

- If you started at age twenty-five, you would end up with more than $1 million
- If you started at age forty-five, you'd end up with around $200,000

It's not just that waiting to forty-five means missing twenty years of payments. A straight calculation shows that is a difference of $100,000. But most of what makes the difference between starting at twenty-five and waiting until forty-five is in compound interest—the money generated by your money over time. The longer you make steady contributions, the more you earn in compound interest. This means every month you wait to begin saving *costs you money*.

We travel through life assuming we'll have more money to invest after we reach a certain stage. But then something unexpected occurs, and the goal of saving more money never happens.

The next thing we know, it feels too late to do anything. But the reality is, it's never too late to get started.

If you start planning late, though, you will have to face one or more of the following consequences:

- You will have to save more money now
- You will have to delay your retirement
- You will have to reduce your standard of living in retirement
- You will have to find work or other sources of income after retirement

Obviously, you want to minimize these negative effects, which is why it's important to take action now.

You may be able to take advantage of opportunities to restructure your investments or claim tax relief from previous years. Many of our clients have been surprised at how we've been able to help them make up for missed time.

Key Factors in Retirement Planning

One of the main reasons planning for retirement can be difficult is the many different factors you need to consider.

Here are just a few you need to think about before you even start to consider how much money you'll need to save:

- **Health care:** The costs keep on rising, and it becomes more and more difficult to meet them in your senior years as your chances of needing care are higher. We'll talk about this in more detail later.

- **Inflation:** While it's been less of a concern in recent years compared to the past, who knows what will happen in the future?

*Even inflation of just 1 or 2 percent a year
can make a big dent in your savings over time.*

• **Low interest rates:** While future interest rates are unpredictable, interest rates on savings have been very low in recent years.

This has been a particular problem for people at or near retirement who typically prefer more conservative investment options.

• **Longevity:** While none of us can know or predict how long we will live, the average life span has been steadily increasing over time.

People in previous generations did not live many years after retirement, but people today are living into their eighties, nineties, and beyond. This means retirement savings may have to last many years.

• **Liquidity:** There are many reasons why you might need access to significant amounts of money—whether for predictable factors, such as college fees and family weddings, or for less predictable events.

You have to consider when you might want access to your money and what the costs and tax implications of that might be.

• **Taxation:** Paying tax creates potentially the largest financial commitment at all stages of your life. Therefore, it's important to plan so you don't pay more to Uncle Sam than necessary.

In our experience, too many people fail to take taxes into account when planning their retirement income needs. Remember, it's not necessarily what you make, but what you keep determines your standard of living in retirement.

- **Social Security:** You need to calculate how to extract the maximum benefit you are entitled to from Social Security.

Getting this one decision right could potentially mean thousands of additional dollars in retirement income for you.

- **Wealth transfer:** You need to find the most tax-efficient method to transfer assets to your heirs. Otherwise, Uncle Sam could end up as your biggest beneficiary!

- **Family protection:** While your children or grandchildren may not be your financial responsibility in your golden years, you will want to ensure your spouse or partner is cared for if they are left on their own. Otherwise, he or she could end up losing some of their income if you pass away first.

Some people also need to ensure they have provisions to provide care for dependents, such as a special needs child.

That's why life insurance and family protection can still be relevant later in life. It can also play a role in tax planning. We'll talk more about that later.

- **Attitude to risk:** The potential returns you will receive on your money depend on how much risk you are willing to take with it. That's why you need to take your attitude toward risk into account when planning, something we'll discuss in detail later on.

- **Long-term care needs:** Our planning for retirement must take into account the possibility of needing special care at some stage.

This can be extremely concerning and very expensive if not planned for properly. Even assistance with basic needs, such as bathing and getting dressed, can be expensive. So be sure to include these costs in your overall retirement planning.

- **Planned retirement age:** The age at which you plan to retire will have a considerable impact on how much money you need.

Retiring later means you have more time to save and will have a shorter period to dig into your funds.

- **Desired lifestyle in retirement:** What you want to do in retirement will determine how much money you need.

Many people underestimate what they will need to spend each day. You might think you will spend less, but often we see people find they actually spend more.

As you can see, there are numerous challenges facing the retirees of today.

We'll dive into these elements in detail as we go through the book. So, let's keep moving forward.

KEY #2

Navigating Comfortably Up and Down the Retirement Mountain

A key component of a happy retirement is knowing you will always have the income and resources you need to live the lifestyle you want.

In your working years, you usually build your lifestyle based on what you earn from employment or your own business, perhaps combined with other sources such as investment income or inheritance.

Even when your income is variable, the concept usually stays fairly straightforward, and you can predict your lifestyle for some time into the future.

In retirement, however, the situation is often more complex.

For example:
- You don't know how long you are going to live.
- Your income may depend on financial conditions.
- You may have limited opportunities to increase your income.
- Your income depends on factors outside your control.
- Your needs for income may be unpredictable (e.g., due to health issues).

Therefore, one of the concepts we talk about in the process of planning your retirement is "replacing your paycheck."

You must ensure you have some stability and predictability to your income. This can also be a challenge for the aforementioned reasons.

That's why we encourage people not to think of retirement as being a destination in its own right, but rather as the start of a new phase in your personal and financial life, which needs careful planning.

> **In your working years, you can usually predict your lifestyle for some time into the future.**

There's quite a lot of complicated information to plow through in this segment, so we've tried to keep it high-level without drilling down too far into technical detail.

In practice, everybody has different needs and is at different stages in life, so we'll identify the over-arching, common issues and leave it to you and your advisor to then drill down specifics on an individual basis.

In this chapter, we will cover the following:

- The Retirement Mountain: Two Phases of Planning
    - Retirement Income Stool: The Three Legs
    - Factors Influencing Your Retirement Lifestyle
    - Understanding the Difference Between Accumulation and Distribution

- Accumulation Phase: Keys to Maximization
    - Tax Buckets
    - Risk Buckets
    - Diversification

- Distribution Phase: Keys to Maximization
    - Making the Money Last
    - Matching Assets to Income Needs
    - Income Choices
    - Using Annuities
    - Selling Other Assets

Let's focus on each of these factors individually.

The Retirement Mountain: Two Phases of Planning

We like to think of planning for retirement as being similar to climbing a mountain.

Successfully planning for retirement can be a challenging task, and the mountain climbing example seems like an especially appropriate analogy. Like mountaineering, planning for retirement is best done with a good map and an experienced guide.

> *Planning for retirement is best done with a good map and an experienced guide.*

Climbing a mountain involves two stages, the ascent and the descent, and these phases require different approaches.

Now, you may think the most challenging part of climbing a mountain is the ascent and, once you reach the top, coming down is the easy part.

However, here's the reality:

> *Most mountain climbing accidents occur on the descent.*
>
> *By some estimates, 80 percent of all climbing injuries and deaths happen on the way down, after the climbers successfully reached the top.*

In our experience, this analogy has an equal application to retirement planning.

> *Too many people put their focus on planning for the day they retire and don't spend enough time planning for the life ahead after they retire.*

As with mountaineering, the steps you need to take on the ascent—the period leading up to retirement—are very different from those you need to take on the descent—the rest of your life.

The first phase of retirement planning (the ascent) is known as the **accumulation phase.**

The second phase (the descent) is the **distribution phase**.

In the accumulation phase, your priorities are pretty straightforward: Set aside as much money as you can and watch it grow as much as possible.

In the distribution phase, your priorities are very different and more complex.

One of the most important elements in retirement is achieving the best possible income. At the same time, you need to take steps to protect your assets and ensure they continue to grow.

Ideally, you want to do this while paying as little tax as possible, and while also thinking about providing financial security for your loved ones.

So, you can begin to see, just as you wouldn't set off on a mountaineering expedition without careful planning for both the ascent and descent, you need to take time to do the same for both financial phases of your retirement planning.

So, let's start the "wrong way around" and look at the second phase first.

Retirement Income Stool: The Three Legs

In planning for the descent phase (the distribution), a good way to visualize your income situation after retirement is to view it as a three-legged stool.

The three legs are:

- Social Security
- Pension
- Retirement savings

A happy and comfortable retirement has historically depended on all three legs.

In a sense, the three legs are the elements that will make up the retirement "paycheck" we mentioned earlier.

Of course, the three legs probably won't be the same size, and the importance of each will vary from one person to another.

For example, in some cases, the Social Security leg will be paramount, while for others, it will be less central.

However, the key to creating the best retirement strategy possible depends on receiving the most you can get out of all three legs.

The truth is, we want everyone to collect the most they can from the Social Security leg, and making the right, informed choices could be worth many thousands of dollars in your retirement years.

Given the importance of this, we cover the Social Security income leg separately in the next chapter.

You also need to get the best out of the first two legs, and that's what we'll cover in this chapter.

Factors That Influence Your Retirement Lifestyle

Let's start by looking more closely at the key factors that will determine your retirement lifestyle.

- **How much you have built up in your retirement fund**

Clearly, one of the most important influences on your retirement paycheck will be how much you have built up in your various retirement funds.

The more you have built up, the more options you will have for the retirement income you want.

- **Other investment assets available**

If you have other assets available aside from just a 401(k) or IRA or other retirement-specific accounts, this can help your retirement income.

This may include having a large house with lots of equity. In this case, if you want to move to a smaller home later, you could hold on to some or all of your home equity and convert it into a retirement income generation component. This area may also include other assets or investments you can rely on.

For example, you may be able to draw income from assets such as a second property you own or dividends from stocks, etc.

These investments may also provide security to fall back on if a sudden emergency or need arises.

• Social Security record

Many people tend to think they don't want to rely too much on their Social Security benefits in their retirement years, but these benefits can be an important part of your planning.

If you have a complete Social Security contributions record (at least forty quarters of income in your lifetime), it can make a notable difference in the amount of income you will receive, as well as in the amount you need to save. Social Security may also provide a certain level of reliable income, allowing for more flexibility with your investment choices.

In the end, Social Security benefits can play an important part in income for many people in their retirement years. Because Social Security is a reliable income stream, it can play a significant role in allowing you more flexibility with your investment choices.

• Attitude to risk

The amount of money you can accumulate for retirement depends, to a large extent, on how your funds are invested.

Generally, if you are willing to take more risk, you have the chance to build up larger assets (though risk means the value, of course, is not guaranteed). However, if you prefer to opt for very conservative investments, your money will build with less speed, and you may need to invest more to make up the difference.

While attitude to risk is important in building up your investment funds, it arguably becomes even more important the closer you move toward and into retirement. It can influence the types of investment you choose, and it can also influence the level of income you wish to withdraw from them.

- **Your desired retirement income**

The size of the portfolio you need to build up also depends on the kind of lifestyle you want to live in your retirement years.

Some people are comfortable with the idea of living a quieter life, while others spend their working lives looking forward to a retirement lived to the fullest, with every day spent on activities they couldn't do while employed—and that usually requires money.

- **Amount you can continue to set aside to invest**

If you haven't fully retired yet, the more money you can put aside for retirement, the larger your fund will be, and the sooner you will be able to retire if you prefer.

You don't have to put all your money into options where you can't access them (i.e., you don't have to limit your savings to 401(k) and related vehicles), but the more you save now, the better off you will be later.

- **How long you think you will live**

Of course, none of us knows exactly how long we will live. But we can often get an idea from our family history and our own health background as to whether it may be many years or just a few.

While you can never tell for certain, this can offer you a useful guide in making some important decisions.

• View of inflation

Inflation can eat away at your savings over the years—whether little by little or suddenly. That's why you need to plan your income in a way that ensures it will continue to grow year by year.

• Your plans for retirement

A key factor influencing the retirement funds you need is whether you have plans for what you are expecting to do in retirement.

For example, many people want to continue working one way or another, and this may mean continued income (though it can also mean additional costs if you decide, for example, to set up a business).

• Your employment situation

Your options for continuing to add to your retirement fund will depend on whether you are currently employed, self-employed, or a business owner.

This will also determine the types of retirement plans available to you (and whether you have the option of employer contributions to help you build up funds faster).

• Other sources of income

Your choices are also influenced by any other sources of income you might have in retirement.

For example, many people take on other jobs in retirement. This can influence your Social Security benefits and your tax situation, so it requires careful planning.

The Difference Between Accumulation and Distribution

In thinking ahead to retirement, it's important to understand the distinction we've already made between the accumulation phase and the distribution phase.

We've talked about this being like the ascent and descent of a mountain. Another way to visualize it is like a game of football.

Halfway through a game of football, the score has limited relevance. It's only the score at the end of the game that determines who won.

So, what has this got to do with retirement?

As we've already discussed:

• The first half of the retirement game is building your retirement funds—the accumulation phase.

• The second happens when you either spend your money in retirement or pass it on to your loved ones after death—the distribution phase.

Too many people think that just building up a large fund of money is the name of the game.

They reach retirement with sizeable assets and feel it is a job well done. They think they've saved all the money they need for their retirement.

That can be a big mistake.

In reality, they are only at the mid-point of the journey, and, like in football, the winner is determined at the end of the game—when you have enjoyed the level of income you wanted throughout your retirement.

So, at retirement, as in football, you need to remember you have not reached the endpoint of your journey. You are only halfway to your destination. And, as in football, the risk actually increases as time goes on and nears the end.

If your opponents score points early, you have time to claw back into the lead. But, if they pull ahead in the final minutes, it's much harder to make a comeback.

In retirement, you need to be aware of the different risks to consider during accumulation versus distribution.

Let's explain it first with a simple example, and then we'll dive into a more detailed one to highlight the important points.

Let's say you have $100,000 invested. This year you incur a 50 percent loss. Next year you incur a 50 percent gain.

Many people think this means they are back to where they started with the $100,000.

In fact, you only have $75,000.

How can this be so?

You lost 50 percent of the $100,000. This leaves you with $50,000, but the following year, you only gained 50 percent of the $50,000 you were left with, leaving you with $75,000.

The reality is, it takes a higher gain than your original loss to offset the loss moving forward.

In this example, you would have to make a 100 percent gain the next year in order to offset the earlier 50 percent loss and get you back to your original investment amount.

Let's look at a more detailed example. We have two investors, Investor A and Investor B. They both start in the accumulation phase and then move into the distribution phase.

Accumulation Phase

At the start of the accumulation phase, the investors are both thirty-seven years old, and they're going to work until they're sixty-five.

They both start out with $100,000 each, and we will apply the actual historical returns of the S&P 500 from 1980 to 2008 to both their portfolios.

However, to make it interesting, we apply the returns in the actual order from 1980 to 2008 for Investor A.

But, for Investor B, we actually flip the returns and apply them in the reverse order. Thus, the 2008 return is applied for 1980, the 2007 return is applied for 1981, etc.

In this scenario, both investors will receive the same annual returns, but those returns will simply be attained in a different order. Now, note the 2008 return was actually -38.49 percent. That was during the depths of the financial crisis.

What's really interesting is, when you look at the total returns for both investors at the end of the accumulation phase, they're exactly the same: $836,000.

How does that work?

When you're living off of your wages and not funding your lifestyle from your retirement accounts, you're not taking any money out. You're only putting money in, and the total return over the period is the same, irrespective of the order of the annual returns.

That's the accumulation phase.

Distribution Phase

Let's fast forward to the distribution phase. The same investors, A and B, carried forward their $836,000.

Just like the accumulation phase, we will apply the same scenario of actual stock market returns from 1980 to 2008 in the actual order they happened to Investor A, and apply the same returns but in reverse order to Investor B.

In addition, this time around, both investors need to take out $50,000 a year (with 3 percent increases to account for inflation) for income to live on because their wages are gone.

This time around, it's a very different outcome.

Investor A (following the actual order of the returns) is able to take out all this income for about a twenty-eight-year period and still have more than $2 million remaining in the account.

Investor B, however, (following the returns in reverse order) runs out of money in about ten years.

How did that happen?

How did they make the same amount in the accumulation phase but have such different results when they were in the distribution phase?

It all comes down to what happens in the first four or five years after you climb over the mountain and start dipping into the distribution phase.

The first four or five years are the most critical.

If you take a big hit right away in the early years, it can make a huge difference to your retirement income and, ultimately, your retirement overall.

For instance, someone who retired in 2008 and suffered a 38.94 percent reduction in the value of their assets in year one (and still had to take out the $50,000 to live) will take a long time to recover, and they may suffer a significant drop in their standard of living.

The truth is, it's very hard to recover from something like that—both mathematically and emotionally!

Now, of course, that's a very dramatic example. It's rare to have such a huge drop in one year. But it did actually happen, and large drops in market value can certainly occur from time to time.

The reason we explain this is to illustrate the difference between the two distinct phases of your financial life. Both have to be addressed differently.

If something like this happens around the time you retire, it can make a big difference in your retirement plans, and you must manage the risk and plan accordingly.

Accumulation Phase: Keys to Maximization

One of the most important issues in planning for retirement is ensuring your funds are invested in the right way to provide the retirement paycheck you want.

The question most often asked is, "Where should I invest my money?"

It would be great if there was a simple solution to that problem, but the reality is it depends on many factors, such as your age, your income, your current circumstances, and your own attitude to important considerations, such as risk and freedom of access to your money.

Some helpful rules of thumb exist, such as making as much use as possible of retirement plans such as 401(k)s and IRAs.

But always remember a 401(k) or an IRA is not, in and of itself, a plan for your retirement. It is simply one of the vehicles to get you there.

So, it's important to get a good understanding of how everything fits in the overall picture.

The bottom line is, if you have set aside $10,000 for your retirement, you want that $10,000 to have grown as much as possible by the time you are ready to draw on it.

Three main factors determine how this works out:

- The **tax** you pay on the growth and income.
- The **risk** you are willing to take with the money invested—which will affect the potential return you get (i.e., the income and growth).
- The **diversification** in your portfolio across different types of investments.

Each of these is, to some extent, within your control.

Clearly, you can't determine exactly what your returns will be many years into the future, but the choices you make throughout the process—both before and after retirement—will help determine what effect these factors have on them.

> **The best option can depend on a wide range of factors and on your personal preferences.**

We'll get into talking about the different types of investments later, but it's a good idea to start by thinking about your investment options as "buckets." You choose which bucket is best for your needs at any time.

The right buckets for you will vary over time, and you will usually want to include a mix of different buckets in your overall strategy.

The two main types of buckets we look at are:

- Tax buckets
- Risk buckets

Understanding the Tax Buckets

The first set of buckets is based on taxation. There are essentially three ways you can be taxed, and this leads to three different tax buckets:

- Tax Now
- Tax-Deferred
- Tax-Free

Let's look at the differences between them when you have set aside $10,000 from your employment income in a year, and you want to put it toward your retirement.

1. "Tax Now" Bucket

The first way to save your money is in the Tax Now Bucket.

Uncle Sam will start by taking a bite out of your initial $10,000 as income tax. Let's just say for the example you are in the 24 percent income tax bracket. So, Uncle Sam will take 24 percent, and you are left with $7,600 to invest.

If you then go on and earn 10 percent on the $7,600, you will have a $760 gain in the first year.

Uncle Sam now steps in again and wants his share of the gain. He asks you to send 15 percent of the gain for what we call the capital gains tax—or $114.

So, you started with $10,000 and ended up with a gain of $646.

This approach, if used with all of your money, may not help you be retirement ready in the best way possible. That's not to say you should never have money in this bucket, but it's not likely to be the core element of your strategy.

2. "Tax-Deferred" Bucket

The second type of tax bucket you may invest in is the Tax-Deferred Bucket.

This bucket generally consists of the main retirement plans, such as 401(k)s, IRAs, etc.

However, it's important to remember these are just labels based on the tax laws. They are not actual types of investments. The labels simply reflect the parts of the tax code that determine how and when you are to be taxed.

You may have heard these plans being called "qualified," which simply means they comply with the tax laws and are therefore eligible to provide tax advantages.

Let's see how our $10,000 would be treated in this bucket.

As a qualified plan, the investment is made before your income tax is calculated, so the full $10,000 is invested.

Your investment may also grow free of taxes, so let's apply the same return of 10 percent on the $10,000. You would then have a $1,000 gain.

However, because Uncle Sam has let you off the hook during the accumulation phase, he will want his share when you are retired. So, if you draw the money in retirement, it will normally be taxed as income at whatever your normal rate of income tax is at the time of withdrawal. For the case of this example, let's say that's 24 percent, so Uncle Sam takes $240 from you.

So here, you started with $10,000 and ended up with a gain of $760.

Uncle Sam will also require you to take at least a minimum amount of money each year from your traditional tax-deferred plans, such as IRAs and 401(k)s when you turn seventy-two. This is the required minimum distribution, or RMD. For many years, RMDs began by the April following when the account holder turned age seventy-and-one-half. The SECURE Act, which took effect on January 1, 2020, pushed the age to begin RMDs back to seventy-two. It also allowed investors to continue making contributions to IRA or 401(k) plans; prior to the SECURE Act, investors had to stop all contributions at seventy-and-one-half.

3. "Tax-Free" Bucket

The third way to save your money is what we will call the Tax-Free Bucket. With this approach, your money may grow free of taxes, like in an IRA and 401(k), but you can also take your money out tax-free.

However, bear in mind, unlike the tax-deferred strategy, your initial investment is paid from your after-tax income. As you'll see here, sometimes it's better to pay the tax upfront and benefit from having the funds tax-free later.

> **There is nothing more demoralizing than a small but adequate income.**
>
> **Edmund Wilson**

There are currently three ways you can withdraw money tax-free. These include:

- Municipal bonds
- Roth IRA
- Life insurance

Let's see how our $10,000 would be treated in this bucket.

Uncle Sam will start by taking a bite out of it as income tax. Let's just say he takes 24 percent, so you are left with $7,600 to invest.

Your investment may grow free of taxes now, so you might be able to earn the same 10 percent return on the $7,600. You would then have a $760 gain.

In this case, Uncle Sam doesn't ask for any more tax.

So, you started with $10,000 and ended up with a return of $760.

Please bear in mind, these are just examples to demonstrate how the different options work.

The exact rates of return and taxes depend on a wide range of factors, and our examples didn't factor in any investment fees, either. So, the right tax bucket for you will depend on your personal circumstances and objectives.

Remember, these options are simply labels that reflect the tax arrangements. They do not relate to how your money is invested as far as the particular products and degrees of risk etc.

We'll talk about how your money is invested and the return you can receive on it in a moment.

First, let's talk some more about the differences between these three options.

Choosing the Right Tax Bucket

As with most of these situations, when it comes to choosing the right bucket, no single answer applies to everyone.

The best option can depend on a wide range of factors and on your personal preferences.

Most people will probably want to have at least some of their money in the Tax Now Bucket.

It doesn't have many of the advantages the other two buckets have, but it usually gives you more flexibility and freedom of access on what to do with your money.

For this reason, it can provide a good home for the funds you may need access to at any time—whether to pay for a family vacation or move to a new house.

It's not easy to put a percentage on how much money you should have in this segment, as it depends partly on the overall value of your savings.

If you have a large amount of savings, you may be able to have a relatively small portion of them in this bucket, so you can take more advantage of the benefits in the others.

> **Make sure you are taking advantage of any employer match available to you.**

When you have funds set aside for flexible access, you can then look at how much you allocate to the other options.

The next priority is to look at how much you are allocating to the Tax-Deferred Bucket.

This allows you to make sure you are taking full advantage of the tax reliefs and benefits available.

In particular, if you are employed, you want to make sure you are taking advantage of any employer match available to you.

As you know, employer matching means your employer makes a contribution to your retirement plan, such as a 401(k), based on the amount of contribution you make.

For example, if they match 50 percent, your employer will contribute $1 for every $2 you contribute, up to a specified limit.

Here are some important things to consider when it comes to employer-sponsored retirement plans:

- An employer match is free money; please take advantage of it.
- If your employer offers a 401(k) plan, use it.
- If they offer matching, maximize it.

Normally, you should contribute as much as you need to receive the full employer matching contribution. Don't let this free money go to waste.

Beyond this, it's a good idea to at least be aware of the maximum you are allowed to contribute to the tax-deferred bucket.

The Tax-Free Bucket (which could also be called the "Taxed-Upfront-and-Then-Never-Again" Bucket) will depend on your personal circumstances. Some people will use it more extensively than others.

How the Main Retirement Plans Fit with the Tax Buckets

Several different types of assets fit into the Tax-Deferred Bucket, depending on your employment status, but the two main types are:

- IRAs—Individual Retirement Accounts are personal plans which individuals open on their own rather than opening through an employer.
- 401(k)s—The 401(k) is a type of retirement plan usually provided by an employer. You cannot open a 401(k) plan as an individual.

While the preceding descriptions of these accounts may appear to be simple, this is really just an overview, and there are variations of each!

For instance, there are different types of IRAs, including:

- Traditional IRAs
- SEP IRAs—For self-employed individuals
- SIMPLE IRAs—For small business owners and self-employed individuals

Each type of IRA has eligibility requirements, including income parameters. They also have annual maximum contribution limits on the amount you can deposit.

The attraction of Traditional IRAs is, as we have discussed, paying the contributions out of your before-tax income—you save tax now.

However, there are some restrictions on how your money can be invested and on how easily you can gain access to it.

> **Working hard to earn more money and then giving it away in higher taxes isn't financially intelligent, even if you do put some of it into a retirement account.**
>
> **Robert Kiyosaki**

Meanwhile, in the 401(k) retirement plan your employer provides, you decide how much you want to contribute to the plan—up to a certain annual maximum. Typically, your employer takes that amount out of your salary, before taxes, and puts it into the account.

You also get to decide how you want your money invested, within certain limits.

For example, your employer's plan may have a selection of investments for you to choose from. You decide how you want to spread out your investments and risk.

When you leave that employer, you keep the money and the account. You might roll it over into your new employer's plan or you can roll it into your IRA. There may be some fees and penalties depending on how you choose to transfer this money.

We believe it's a significant mistake to simply close the account and pocket the cash, because you'll pay taxes as well as a penalty (if you're under age fifty-nine-and-one-half), and the money is no longer working for your retirement years.

Even if your company offers a 401(k), opening an IRA account provides a valuable way to save for retirement. There are two types of personal IRAs. These are the Roth and the Traditional. Let's take a closer look at these.

Roth IRAs vs. Traditional IRAs

With a Roth IRA, you pay taxes on your earnings, but you don't pay taxes when you withdraw the money in the future if you follow the conditions of the account.

Alternatively, Traditional IRA contributions go into the account pre-tax. However, Uncle Sam will tax your withdrawals in retirement.

There are some other differences, too, between Roth and Traditional IRAs. For instance, Roth IRAs allow you to withdraw your contributions without paying a penalty, unlike Traditional IRAs.

However, with both a Roth and a Traditional IRA, you'll be penalized 10 percent for withdrawing any investment earnings before age fifty-nine-and-one-half, unless it's for a "qualifying reason."

The qualifying reasons are serious because they can lead to finances becoming derailed.

The qualifying reasons for taking an IRA distribution penalty-free before age fifty-nine-and-one-half include paying for:

- College expenses for you, your spouse, your children, or even your grandchildren.
- Medical expenses greater than 7.5 percent of your adjusted gross income.
- A first-time home purchase. You can borrow up to $10,000 without penalty.
- The costs of a sudden disability.

(Note: If you convert money from a traditional IRA into a Roth IRA, you can't take it out penalty-free until at least five years after the conversion.)

Many people over their lives build up a range of different plans as their circumstances change. Often, they end up later in life with a number of different savings and investment plans, not all of which may still serve their current needs. Therefore, it's important to review your current plans regularly to ensure they are still appropriate and invested wisely.

We often find that people think they are tied into certain plans for the remainder of their lives. But the reality is, oftentimes, plans can be changed for something better, leading to potential savings in fees and, ultimately, a better retirement.

We're not saying you should have all your eggs in one basket. We're just saying sometimes people have too many baskets that are not right for their current circumstances.

Understanding the Risk Buckets

While identifying the right tax bucket for your investments is important, another key factor that will affect your retirement paycheck is getting the best possible return on your investment.

In order to do this, you need to decide how much risk you are willing to take with your money. To this end, we generally categorize investments into different buckets according to the risk.

The three buckets according to risk are:

- Low Risk
- High Risk
- Medium Risk

Let's look at each:

• Low Risk Bucket

This bucket contains what are traditionally considered "safe" financial options, such as savings accounts, money markets, etc. While this money is typically liquid, the tradeoff to this is the rates are really low—at this time, around 0 to 1percent.

However, these types of accounts can be attractive because they have no risk to your invested capital. But, you may not be keeping up with inflation and, in turn, could run the risk of running out of money during your retirement.

So, while these options can play a vital role in your retirement planning, you probably don't want to put all of your money here.

• High Risk Bucket

This is where you invest directly in the stock market and other higher-return potential financial vehicles, like property, etc.

Stocks share in the profit growth of companies. Their value moves up and down depending on the financial performance of the company and general economic conditions.

The potential returns can be very attractive with stocks, but there is also a high risk you could lose money, as these accounts have no guarantees.

• Medium Risk Bucket

This falls somewhere between the other two buckets and generally offers the opportunity for better returns than having your funds in a cash account (while also posing less risk than more aggressive stock market investments overall).

This category generally includes investments like bonds, which are issued by governments, municipalities, and companies, and pay a set rate of interest.

Their value increases and decreases depending on general economic conditions.

This medium risk category may also include property you own for income or capital growth, whether directly or through an externally managed fund.

(Note: Property can also sometimes be in the higher risk category, depending on the actual investment.)

Usually your investment strategy will include some elements of all three buckets.

Factors Determining Your Approach

A number of factors will help determine the right approach for you. These include:

• Attitude to Risk

Some people are more willing to take risks with their money than others, so the right options for you will depend on your personal feelings about risk.

• Diversification

A good investment portfolio spreads out into different types of investments and asset classes.

You wouldn't want to put all your money in stocks or in one type of stock. And while diversification can't ensure a profit or guarantee you won't lose money, it helps reduce your overall risk if one investment declines sharply.

- **Timing**

Your choices will depend on how close you are to the date you will need or want to take out the money.

If you need the money soon, you likely will choose less risky, more liquid, investments.

If you are able to leave it invested longer, you will have the chance for higher returns.

- **Fees**

You also need to consider the cost of investing as part of your calculation.

So, what is the best option for you?

Clearly, we can't say what's right for everybody, and it's important for you to review your current plans and consider whether they need to be changed.

Diversification for Risk and for Taxes

One of the keys to managing risk is understanding the importance of diversification.

There's no doubt one of the keys to achieving the right type and amount of diversification is being an informed investor.

Informed investors understand market diversification is a good strategy to deal with the often-volatile marketplace.

Getting diversification right has the potential to help you see increased stock market returns by allowing you to manage your risk across a number of different investments.

Let's talk about what we mean by diversification.

Here's how diversification is defined by Investopedia.com:

> "A risk management technique that mixes a wide variety of investments within a portfolio.
>
> "The rationale behind this technique contends that a portfolio of different kinds of investments will, on average, yield higher returns and pose a lower risk than any individual investment found within the portfolio.
>
> "Diversification strives to smooth out unsystematic risk events in a portfolio so that the positive performance of some investments will neutralize the negative performance of others.
>
> "Therefore, the benefits of diversification will hold only if the securities in the portfolio are not perfectly correlated."

Okay, that's a bit of a mouthful.

Perhaps a simpler definition you'd hear from a financial professional would be something like:

> *Spreading your dollars among different asset classes.*

Well, this is a little less confusing, but what exactly do we mean by "asset class"?

Again from Investopedia.com, an asset class is defined as:

> *"A group of securities that exhibit similar characteristics, behave similarly in the marketplace, and are subject to the same laws and regulations."*

Here are some common examples of generic asset classes:

- Protected principal
- Income
- Growth and income
- Growth
- Aggressive growth

Examples of more specific asset classes and categories are:

- Cash or cash-equivalent Treasury bonds
- Government bonds
- Corporate bonds
- High-yield (junk bonds)
- Stocks
- Large-cap or small-cap stocks
- International investments
- REITs
- Natural resources
- Precious metals
- Foreign currency

Each asset class is expected to:

- Reflect different risk characteristics
- Reflect different return characteristics
- Perform differently in any given market environment

One of the keys to a more successful portfolio is having the appropriate mix of different asset classes.

One key challenge is that no one knows which asset class will perform best over any given period of time.

We know we can't control the stock market, we know we can't control income tax brackets, and we know we can't control the state tax rates.

However, to a certain extent, we can control the amount of money the income tax and state tax rates apply against us. Thus, your investments should also be diversified to help maximize your assets based upon your individual tax situation.

It's why we believe considering the importance of being diversified just as important for taxes as it is for return.

Many financial professionals recognize the importance of diversification for return purposes, but often we see other people in our field who don't account for the significance of taxes when it comes to different asset classes.

The key is to find the right level of diversification both for tax and for return purposes.

For instance, you may want to explore some financial vehicles designed to fill the void between stock market investments and lower-yielding interest accounts.

If you haven't already done so, you should perform an independent analysis of your potential taxes in your financial plan.

Distribution Phase: Keys to Maximization

The risks mentioned previously have an even greater impact when you move beyond your initial retirement date, so it's important to plan for that in the right way.

The problem we often see is many retirees or soon-to-be retirees don't know what their plan is, and they often don't actually have a plan at all.

The result is many retirees outlive their income. This is something we want to avoid.

Managing Your Investments to Last in Retirement

When you are already in retirement, the principles for managing your investments are the same as the ones we discussed earlier in this segment.

You will be interested in the potential returns while also taking into account the levels of **risk**. You will then take into account the **tax** implications.

> The conclusions you reach in investing your money for retirement may be different from those you reach after retirement.

The conclusions you reach at this stage may be different, however. You may be interested in taking less risk with your investments. Your tax considerations may also be different.

In addition, you will have to factor income into the process. You may well want to take the dividends and income from your investments rather than leave them invested.

You will also have to think about whether you want to draw on the capital from your investments.

Matching Assets to Income Needs

One of the solutions we recommend is something called the Time-Based Segmentation System.

This is a planning tool that aims to reduce concerns about income both now and later by creating and monitoring earmarked accounts for both income and growth.

It creates separate accounts for:

- Short-term income
- Mid-term income
- Long-term income
- Growth

Designed to provide more reliable income in the early years through the use of conservative instruments, a segmented system affords people the ability to shift riskier investments to a longer-term portfolio.

Short-term income, the first phase, focuses on guaranteed income. It uses financial vehicles that have a much higher level of protection.

Mid-term income, the second phase of this plan, focuses on principal protection, much like the first phase, but has a somewhat longer timeframe before the income begins, allowing the strategy to rely on financial vehicles that have slightly higher growth rates.

Long-term income is the third phase. This phase represents income sources that won't be used for eight to twelve years after retirement. This longer waiting period gives the investor the opportunity to use products with potentially higher rates of return, depending on the investor's risk tolerance.

Since it is earmarked for income down the road, one may consider using financial vehicles that carry lower risk or repositioning vehicles with higher risk the closer one gets to needing this income.

Finally, the last phase of the strategy is the growth component. By addressing ten to twenty years of income up front, some investors may feel more comfortable with assuming more risk in this section in an effort to hopefully achieve higher growth and replenishment of their portfolio.

This strategy is referred to as the Time-Based Segmentation System because of how it reflects the changing needs in the various phases.

When the short-term income account is consumed, the mid-term income account will replace it. From there, the long-term income account will shift over and become the mid-term account. As the growth account accumulates, assets will slowly shift over to replenish the depleting accounts and continue the cycle.

Two other components of the System are known as the Protection Umbrella and a Legacy Transfer Bucket.

The **Protection Umbrella** is where one might address any long-term care insurance needs in order to protect the portfolio from this risk.

The **Legacy Transfer Bucket** is where one may look at instruments and strategies to most efficiently transfer assets and legacy to the beneficiaries of choice.

Note that each client situation is different, and each Time-Based Segmentation System must be tailored to meet the unique needs of each client.

The concept strives to reduce risk by earmarking and allocating assets for different needs in retirement.

The Income You'll Get from Your Retirement Plans

If you are lucky enough to have traditional retirement plans providing benefits linked to your earnings, such as a company pension, you have many advantages.

One of the most significant is you can look forward to certain payments for the rest of your life.

However, there are decisions you need to make at the start, including choosing between:

Pension: Regular payment for life

Lump-Sum: Single payment to invest and provide income

When you choose the pension option, you have to make choices to determine what income, if any, will be provided for your dependents after your death.

Many people are tempted to take the lump sum because they prefer the flexibility, but some pension arrangements provide regular increases in line with the cost of living.

However, it's important to look at the numbers and to get good advice that can help you make the right choices.

Using Annuities to Provide a Retirement Income

One of the biggest challenges of managing your money during retirement is you don't know how long it needs to last.

However, one way you can create some certainty in your income is through the use of annuities.

In its simplest form, an annuity is an arrangement between you and an insurance company where the insurance carrier pays out a set amount of income in exchange for your payment of a specific lump sum.

The challenge with annuities is often that the practice is not as straightforward as the theory.

For instance, there are many different kinds of annuities with many variations on the types of income they can provide, as well as in the way they are taxed.

Broadly, annuities can be split into different categories based on when the income from them is paid.

Immediate: With an immediate annuity, you start receiving the income as soon as you make the payment. (Income here will typically begin within six to twelve months of purchasing the annuity.)

Deferred: With a deferred annuity, the income is paid starting at some agreed date in the future.

Annuities can also be split as follows, depending on what happens during their accumulation phase:

> **The attraction of annuities is they can provide a degree of certainty to your income.**

Fixed: With fixed annuities, you receive the same amount of income (whether paid monthly, quarterly, or yearly) for the full period.

One limitation of fixed annuities is your payments don't normally increase over time, meaning their purchasing power reduces every year based on inflation. This can prove significant, even in periods of relatively low inflation, as your living expenses will still tend to rise over time.

A variation of the fixed annuity allows cost-of-living protection to be built in.

This means payments will start at a lower level and have the potential to increase each year on a pre-arranged basis—perhaps increasing a set amount each year or linking to inflation.

The advantage of the fixed annuity approach is the income you receive stays predictable.

Variable: With a variable annuity, the amount of income you receive depends partly on the performance of underlying investment assets.

While this could lead to higher income when stock markets perform well, it has a higher level of risk, too, as your income could significantly reduce if markets perform badly.

Indexed Annuity: A variation of the regular fixed annuity is the indexed annuity.

Here, the amount of income you receive is linked to a stock market index rather than containing or relying on underlying stocks.

> **One of the biggest challenges of managing your money during retirement is you don't know how long it needs to last.**

With this annuity, you earn interest tied to an external index while never being invested in the market. (The interest is limited by the insurance company, so you won't typically earn all of the gains of the index.)

This usually includes a level of protection, so values do not fall when stock markets fall. An advantage here is that you'll typically see your value increase by more than that of a fixed annuity, but you won't have the risks of being actually invested in the stock market.

Yet another consideration with annuities is the contract's term of payment.

Life: An annuity may be paid for your whole life and cease at your death. (Some annuities may also pay out an income stream for your spouse or partner for the remainder of their lives, too.)

Fixed-Term: With a fixed-term income payout, the annuity income will cease after a set number of years.

Another factor to consider is what happens to the annuity payment upon death. For example, it may:

- Cease immediately upon death.
- Continue to dependents for the remainder of a fixed period (for example, if the fixed period was twenty years and you die after twelve years, an annuity will continue to your spouse or other dependents for the remaining eight years).
- Continue for the lifetime of the surviving spouse.

The wide range of options means it's extremely important you find the right kind of advice before making any decisions about annuities.

Nevertheless, they can play a central role in planning your retirement income.

The attraction of annuities is they can provide a degree of certainty to your income, as the guarantees they offer are backed by the financial strength of the issuing insurance company.

On the downside, you have to make decisions early on about the type of income you want, and these decisions are difficult to change later. Also, you will pay penalties if you need to take income out in the early years of the contract.

For example, if you live only for a short period after retirement, your dependents could be worse off if you have not chosen an annuity that caters to them.

Equally, you will likely receive a lower income if you choose a policy that provided good benefits for your spouse and/or dependents.

The amount of annuity income you will receive depends on such factors as your age, gender, and the amount you put in the contract to begin with.

In general, the older you are when you start the annuity income payout, the higher the income you will receive for the same amount of money.

You may also receive a higher income if you have health issues that reduce your life expectancy.

Choosing between immediate annuities is relatively easy because insurers will provide you with quotes of the monthly repayments based on a specific investment.

However, choosing the right type of annuity is extremely important and it's therefore important to get good advice.

Increasing Your Paycheck by Selling Assets

As we discussed earlier, many people make the assumption they will be able to live less expensively in retirement—some think they will be able to live off the proceeds of selling assets, such as their home.

This may well apply, but, often, it is not as clear-cut as people expect it to be.

Although you may lose some of the costs part of everyday life when you were working, there will be other costs that arise in retirement—often because you will have more time to spend money!

There are many, many factors, and all of them must work together for your benefit.

For instance, you may find you don't want to sell your house in retirement, and it may not even be possible. You also have to take tax considerations into account as another significant factor in the decision to sell real estate assets.

As this chapter has demonstrated, there are a variety of options available when it comes to funding retirement and establishing income. But there is no single account, product, or financial vehicle that can replace having a well-thought-out strategy for investing and taking income in a way that is coordinated, strategic, and efficient for inflation and taxes.

For a real-life example of what we mean, check out the following case study.

Case Study: Mia and Walt

When we first met Mia and Walt, they were both age sixty. They had about $900,000 in retirement and brokerage accounts, $150,000 in savings, and no mortgage on their home. Their kids were grown, and they were on their own.

Both Mia and Walt were at the point where they wanted to slow down over the course of the next two years and perhaps start collecting Social Security at age sixty-two.

Their main problem was they had fourteen accounts with no clear pattern or connection to each other. They had a financial hodgepodge pieced together by salesmen who put them in everything under the sun—except a decent plan!

Their goal was simple: to withdraw $2,500/month in year one, $3,500/month in year two, and $4,500/month in year three and beyond.

They didn't have a clue on how to coordinate all these accounts into a plan allowing them to create a steady stream of income for the rest of their lives while keeping up the lifestyle they were used to.

The challenges Mia and Walt were facing are ones we see frequently. Many people save any way they can, and they have saved in whatever is available. But a pile of unrelated, uncoordinated assets with no strategy isn't a great way to maximize your potential income.

Instead, we help people consolidate where it makes sense and use different efficient accounts in various combinations to establish the optimal income distribution.

What We've Learned in This Chapter

Retirement consists of two distinct phases—like ascending and descending a mountain. First, the **accumulation** phase, then the **distribution** phase.

The distribution phase is like a three-legged retirement income stool. The three legs include:

- Social Security
- Pension
- Personal retirement savings

The way your investments are taxed depends on which tax "bucket" you choose to invest in. These buckets include:

- Tax now
- Tax-deferred
- Tax-free

You can choose several different types of retirement plans depending on your situation. But, remember, having individual assets or investment vehicles (such as a 401(k)) is not the same as having an overall plan for your retirement.

The return you receive on your investments is influenced by the risks you are willing to take. There are essentially three risk levels:

- Low risk
- High risk
- Medium risk

Checklist: Navigating the Retirement Mountain

√ Have you considered how much risk you are willing to take with your investments in order to potentially increase your income in retirement?

√ Do you know how the different sources of retirement income you have will be taxed?

√ Are you relying on selling various assets to provide an income in retirement, and are you confident this is realistic?

√ Do you know what choices you will have to make with your pension plans at retirement—for example, choosing between lump sums and pension income?

√ Have you worked out how much you can afford to put aside each month for your retirement?

√ Are you taking advantage of all the tax benefits available to you in planning for retirement?

√ Are the plans you have consistent with the retirement lifestyle you want?

√ Are the plans you have consistent with your attitude to risk?

KEY #3

Ways to Help You Achieve the Best Social Security Benefits Possible

"If I apply for early Social Security, I get this. If I wait until I only have one life left, I get this."

Many people who have planned ahead for their retirements still don't necessarily view their Social Security benefits as an important part of their financial arrangements.

However, you've probably been contributing to Social Security throughout your working life, and you should be entitled to your share.

Equally, with careful planning, the amounts available can be significant—not just in your own retirement, but also as protection for your loved ones.

Perhaps another reason many people hesitate in making Social Security a key part of their plans is the rules are complicated and making the right choices at various stages can be crucial.

> **Today more people believe in UFOs than believe that Social Security will take care of their retirement.**
>
> **Scott Cook**

So, before you make any important decisions, it's vital to know the right information and advice.

As you read the facts and tips we'll share here, we hope you'll find them useful. No doubt you will also get a sense of the complexity of this decision.

Bear in mind, what you read here cannot possibly cover every situation, since everyone is different.

We'd encourage you to take advantage of the resources provided by the Social Security Administration to reach a better understanding of your own position.

Simply visit **www.ssa.gov**—it's a useful resource to help you understand more about the Social Security program.

What we seek to do here is to shine a light beyond the basic published information in order to cover facts not always publicized by the authorities.

At the end, we hope you'll conclude your Social Security decisions are both important and complex. They should only be made very carefully after taking into consideration all of the factors relevant to your position. We hope you will view us as a valuable resource as you make these important decisions.

We've witnessed numerous situations where individuals and couples were able to significantly increase the total income received from Social Security over their lifetimes (and in support of their loved ones).

So, take the time to become more informed and to hear the right advice.

Here's what we're going to cover in this chapter:

- The History of Social Security
- The Building Blocks of Social Security
- Social Security Choices
- The Retirement Decision
- Spousal Benefits
- Children's Benefits
- Taxation of Social Security
- How Divorce Affects Social Security
- Starting Again If You Make the Wrong Choice
- Getting Advice

The History of Social Security

In order to gain a full understanding of the importance of Social Security, it's useful to understand a bit about the program's history.

The Social Security Act was enacted on August 14, 1935. It was introduced by President Franklin D. Roosevelt as an attempt to limit some of the potential dangers seen at the time in everyday American life, including:

- Old age
- Poverty

- Unemployment
- Widowhood
- Fatherless children

Among the main catalysts for the introduction of Social Security were the stock market crash of 1929 and the Great Depression of the 1930s.

Over the years, needs have changed, so Social Security has been modified and adjusted numerous times.

However, in some ways, the changes to it have been modest in relation to the massive change in the needs of its recipients.

As we discussed at the beginning of this book, there have been major changes in recent years affecting Social Security, such as:

- Changing life expectancy—we live much longer.
- Different employment patterns—few people stay with one employer for life.
- More pensioners—in comparison to people working.
- New options for saving for retirement.
- Huge growth in the costs of health care.

As a result of all these changes, the shape of Social Security will look very different in the future as the cost of the current system has probably become unsustainable.

It's likely the future will see:

- Lower benefits
- Later retirement
- Higher contributions

While those factors are important to take into account, arguably more serious are the rights you have already built up in your life. While nothing is guaranteed, there is, so far, no suggestion that benefits promised in the past will be removed from people who are in or nearing retirement.

Another useful thing to bear in mind is you can't always rely on the Social Security Administration to dispense the most appropriate advice.

No one is saying they aren't helpful or that they try to prevent you from getting benefits.

But the reality is the rules are so complex, and individual circumstances vary so much, the Social Security Administration simply can't provide personalized advice to everyone in every possible scenario.

They are also prohibited by law from giving advice.

> Today there are about 40 million retirees receiving benefits; by the time all the baby boomers have retired, there will be more than 72 million retirees drawing Social Security benefits.
>
> **Tony Snow, Political Commentator**

For example, in response to one of the most common questions asked about Social Security—"When should I take my benefits?"—the Social Security Administration says:

> "There is no one 'best age' for everyone and, ultimately, it is your choice. You should make an informed decision about when to apply for benefits based on your individual and family circumstances."

This statement is, in fact, very true.

Everybody's decision regarding when to take Social Security is a personal one, and it is impossible to predict when will be the best time for any one person to begin receiving Social Security benefits.

Many factors weigh into such a decision, including, but not limited to, your:

- Current health
- Future longevity
- Current financial circumstances
- Marital status
- Age and the age of your spouse
- Earnings capacity today and in the future
- Previous work history
- Desire to retire

Over the next few pages, we'll share some important tips you need to bear in mind.

The Building Blocks of Social Security

To understand your potential Social Security benefits and to make the most of them, there are a few key concepts you need to know.

Age of Eligibility for Social Security

Most people are eligible to start collecting Social Security benefits at age sixty-two. Doing so, however, will reduce the dollar amount you receive, and this reduction will continue for the remainder of your lifetime.

If you wait until your "Full Retirement Age" (FRA—keep reading), you will receive a larger monthly benefit known as your Primary Insurance Amount" (see the following).

If you wait until after you reach your FRA before taking your Social Security pension, your monthly benefit will continue to increase until you reach age seventy.

Primary Insurance Amount (PIA)

Your Primary Insurance Amount, or PIA, is the amount of your Social Security benefit you will receive if you wait until your Full Retirement Age to begin receiving benefits.

Full Retirement Age (FRA)

FRA varies depending on when you were born.

It is age sixty-five for those born in 1937 or earlier and sixty-seven for those born in 1960 or later.

For those born in the years in between, there is a sliding scale according to the following table.

If you were born in:	Your FRA is:
1937 or earlier	65
1938	65 and 2 months
1939	65 and 4 months
1940	65 and 6 months
1941	65 and 8 months
1942	65 and 10 months
1943 – 1954	66
1955	66 and 2 months
1956	66 and 4 months
1957	66 and 6 months
1958	66 and 8 months
1959	66 and 10 months
1960 or later	67

Average Indexed Monthly Earnings (AIME)

The AIME is the formula used by Social Security to determine your PIA.

It is calculated taking into account all of your previous earnings, and it equates them into "today's dollars."

In order to determine your PIA, Social Security calculates your Average Indexed Monthly Earnings during the thirty-five years in which you earned the most.

If you worked less than thirty-five years, those months/years are factored at zero when determining your PIA.

If you are able to work more years or earn more, this should increase your AIME, and therefore your PIA, meaning you will have the prospect of higher benefits.

Social Security Retirement Credits

Credits are a key factor in determining your eligibility to receive Social Security on your own working record, as well as the building blocks for determining how much you will receive.

If you were born in 1929 or later, you need forty credits in order to be eligible for Social Security retirement income benefits.

When you work and pay Social Security taxes, you earn up to a maximum of four "credits" for each year.

The way you earn a credit has changed over the years.

Before 1978, employers reported your earnings every three months, and we called these credits "quarters of coverage" (QCs). You got a QC if you earned at least $50 in a three-month calendar quarter.

In 1978, employers started reporting your earnings just once a year. Since then, credits are based on your total wages and self-employment income during the year, no matter when you did the actual work.

So, you might work all year to earn four credits, or you might earn enough for all four "quarters" (and credits) in a much shorter length of time. The amount of earnings it takes to earn a credit has increased over the years.

In 2020, you must earn $1,410 per "quarter" in covered earnings to get one Social Security or Medicare work credit. This means you need to earn $5,640 to get the maximum four credits for the year.

For more detailed information about this topic or any Social Security facts, visit **www.ssa.gov**.

Delayed Retirement Credits

If you delay retirement beyond your Full Retirement Age, your benefits will be increased by 8 percent per year (calculated as simple interest) until age seventy.

This may appeal to you if you are continuing to work or if you don't currently need the income from Social Security.

Earnings Test

If you work *and* collect Social Security early, you may become subject to the "Earnings Test."

Depending on your age and earnings, Social Security may deduct an amount from your benefits for every dollar you have earned above a certain amount (we will discuss the earnings test in more detail later on).

Provisional Income

Provisional income is measured by your Adjusted Gross Income, excluding Social Security benefits, plus one-half of Social Security benefits.

It is important in calculating your liability to state and federal income tax.

Social Security Benefits Statement

Since 2012, the Social Security Administration has had an online Social Security Statement process.

Previously, you probably received your statement in the mail every year. Social Security will still mail paper statements to workers age sixty and older if they are not already receiving Social Security benefits.

You can always access your most recent statement online at **www.socialsecurity.gov/mystatement**

You have to complete an identification process to verify you are who you say you are. We advise doing this annually to verify your earnings record.

If you discover an error on your earnings record, you are advised to try and have this rectified as soon as possible with the Social Security Administration.

Social Security Choices

Now, since we have these building blocks in place, let's look at some of the key options available and the decisions you must make to receive the best possible benefit out of Social Security for your unique situation.

By the way, there are some 567 different ways to claim your Social Security, so while we can't cover every possible scenario, we will provide some extremely beneficial information.

In addition, note "maximize" does not always mean "to receive the largest monetary amount." The Social Security system provides flexibility because people's needs vary.

The way you take your Social Security benefits will reflect:

Your overall financial situation: If you need the money now, you probably won't want to wait a few more years for a higher amount.

Your marital status: This will affect the benefits available, even if you are divorced or widowed. It may also affect when you want to start taking benefits, e.g., if your spouse is older or younger than you.

Your health: If your health is not good and you are single, you may want to start taking benefits earlier. If you have dependents, you may want to continue working to build up benefits.

Your tax situation: Social Security benefits can be taxable above a certain income threshold, so you may want to defer taking them if your income will be lower in the future.

Your plans for retirement: If you plan to continue working in retirement, you may wish to defer taking benefits.

How long you have been in the workforce: If you have not worked the thirty-five years generally required to receive full benefits, you may want to continue working to build up more entitlements.

Let's look at Social Security benefit decisions in more detail by focusing on the following categories:

- The Retirement Decision
- Spousal Benefits
- Children's Benefits
- Taxation of Social Security
- How Divorce Affects Social Security

The Retirement Decision

Amongst all the complex decisions you have to make about your retirement, you'd like to think the decision on Social Security would be an easy one.

No such luck!

Making the right choices is just as important in this category as in any other. In fact, because your total Social Security benefit could be in the six-figure range (or higher), some people consider Social Security to be one of their top retirement assets.

Also, you have some degree of freedom about when you take your retirement benefits. You can choose to retire at your Full Retirement Age as defined earlier. However, you can choose to start taking your retirement benefits as early as age sixty-two or as late as age seventy.

If you start taking benefits earlier, your benefits will be permanently reduced. If you choose to delay taking benefits, the benefits will be permanently higher.

The way the Social Security Administration has calculated your benefits, your retirement date, whether you file early or late, or even whether you take benefits and pay taxes while still working shouldn't matter all too much—the intention is you will receive the same amount of lifetime benefits.

If you take benefits while working, those taxed benefits will still be credited back in the form of an increased benefit when you reach full retirement age. Whether you delayed or filed early won't make much of a difference for someone of average life expectancy.

BUT WAIT. *Average.*

Your personal life expectancy, health history, and family longevity remain key to determining what benefit is best for you. Although many people start to draw their benefits as soon as they can, there are often significant benefits in waiting. For example, the Social Security Administration estimates:[4]

- More than one in three sixty-five-year-olds today will live to age ninety.
- More than one in seven will live to age ninety-five.

So, if you think you will live longer than average, you could be better off waiting a few years to receive the higher benefit. Equally, if you think you will live less than the average, there may be advantages in retiring earlier.

Of course, nobody knows where they will be in relation to the averages, but the differences are significant. If you wait until age seventy to collect your retirement benefit, your retirement benefit starting at seventy could be roughly 80 percent higher than your age sixty-two retirement benefit.

In the following example, the benefit is $1,320 at age seventy, compared to $750 at age sixty-two.

This higher amount is the result of two factors:

- Your benefits won't receive an Early Retirement Reduction for claiming before your Full Retirement Age

AND

- Your benefits will enjoy earning Delayed Retirement Credits.

---

[4] Social Security. 2019. "Benefits Planner: Life Expectancy." https://www.ssa.gov/planners/lifeexpectancy.html

Remember, you may also receive cost-of-living adjustments each year with Social Security. The table below shows examples of how delaying taking your benefits affects the amount you will receive.

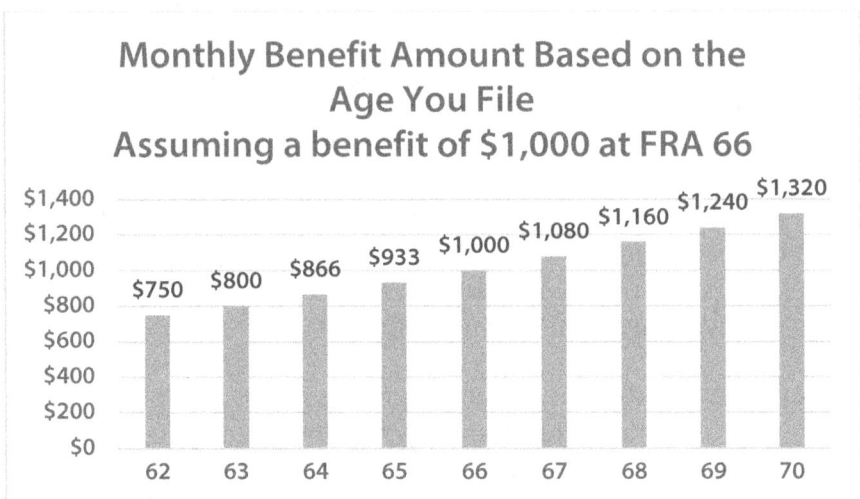

When you look at the chart, you can see every year you delay collecting up to age seventy means you receive an increase of around 8 percent, based on this example. That's not a bad return in today's markets, so it may be worth delaying, depending on your personal choice and circumstances.

Therefore, it's beneficial to consider it carefully and make the right choice.

Another factor to consider in making your decision is any spousal benefits. We'll look at these in more detail later, but, keep in mind, decisions you make can affect your spousal and family benefits.

You also need to think about what happens to your benefits if you continue working after taking your benefits. If you are younger than Full Retirement Age and your earnings exceed a certain amount, your benefits may be restricted. However, your benefits will be increased later to reflect this, so you may still be better off in the long run.

One factor that determines the Social Security benefits you receive is your work history—how long you have been working and how much you have earned. However, by the time you reach retirement, your ability to influence decades of previous earnings history is limited.

You may be able to significantly raise your retirement benefits by continuing to work in your sixties, which could also significantly raise the spousal, child, and other benefits your loved ones collect.

Spousal Benefits

While many people prefer not to rely wholly on Social Security to provide for their retirement, it can be a comfort to know you and your loved ones receive some return on all the contributions you have been paying over the years.

Your spouse and family may be entitled to some benefits even if they have not contributed themselves.

The exact details can be complicated because entitlements depend on your contributions and whether you die before or after you have started taking your Social Security retirement benefits.

Broadly, your family's benefits are based on the Primary Insurance Amount (PIA), which is the amount you would collect at Full Retirement Age (FRA).

The exact amount will depend on your earnings and how many Social Security work credits you earned.

For example, your surviving spouse may be entitled to receive up to 100 percent of your PIA if you die before starting benefits. This will be reduced if they file sometime between age sixty and their own FRA.

If you die after starting your Social Security benefits, your spousal benefits cannot be more than you were receiving.

If your surviving spouse is entitled to Social Security benefits based on their own work record, they can claim whichever benefit is higher—but not both.

If you have enough credits, survivor benefits can be paid to your:

• Spouse (or ex-spouse) who is aged sixty or over (age fifty or older if disabled) provided you were married for at least nine months. An ex-spouse qualifies if married to you for at least ten years provided he or she didn't remarry before age sixty.
• Spouse (or ex-spouse) at any age, if disabled or caring for your child who is under sixteen.
• Unmarried children under eighteen—older if disabled
• Unmarried children under age nineteen if attending elementary or secondary school
• Dependent parents who are age sixty-two or older—in this case, you must have been supplying at least half of their total support

Bear in mind, the rules are complicated and can change, so make sure you receive proper information and advice.

If working out your own Social Security benefits seems complicated enough, it becomes even more complex when you work out the best way to combine both your own and your spouse's benefits (this also applies if you are divorced).

Generally, at age sixty-two, a spouse can choose to take a benefit based on their own work history or on the spouse's, provided the spouse has already filed.

If you are married or divorced, waiting to collect your retirement benefit may not always be in your best interest.

The lower-earning spouse may be better off taking their retirement benefit at age sixty-two and then switching to the spousal benefit, based on their current or ex-spouse's account, starting at Full Retirement Age.

> **Your spouse and family may be entitled to some Social Security benefits even if they have not contributed themselves.**

This can be an important consideration for those who feel their spouse may outlive them and might benefit from a higher survivor benefit after they pass away.

There are various strategies you can use to achieve the best combination of benefits from Social Security.

These strategies can change over time, and they have changed a lot recently, so it's best to seek advice before you make any decisions.

Children's Benefits

If you had children later in life, including adopted children, they can collect benefits up to age seventeen (or age nineteen if they are still in secondary school) if you, your spouse, or ex-spouse are collecting Social Security retirement benefits.

Besides your natural children or adopted children, this could apply to stepchildren, grandchildren, or step-grandchildren under certain circumstances.

Your children can receive survivor benefits if the mother/father of those children died and the children are under age eighteen (or age nineteen if they are still in secondary school).

A maximum family benefit is allowed that applies to the total benefits to you, your spouse, and your children and can be received on your earnings record.

Taxation of Social Security

Under current law, up to 85 percent of Social Security benefits are subject to federal and state income tax, depending on the taxpayer's income.

For taxpayers with provisional incomes less than $25,000 ($32,000 for married joint taxpayers), all Social Security benefits are excluded from taxable income.

For provisional incomes between $25,000 and $34,000 ($32,000 and $44,000 for married joint taxpayers), up to 50 percent of Social Security benefits may be subject to tax.

For those with provisional incomes over $34,000 ($44,000 for married joint taxpayers), up to 85 percent of Social Security benefits may be included in taxable income.

Provisional income is measured by your Adjusted Gross Income, plus one-half of Social Security benefits.

IMPORTANT: These thresholds are NOT indexed for inflation.

This means, unless something changes in the law, eventually the majority of Social Security recipients could be taxed on 85 percent of their Social Security benefits.

It also means you should plan your withdrawals from other accounts carefully.

When it comes to determining whether to pay federal income taxes on your Social Security benefits, withdrawals from Roth IRAs aren't counted, but withdrawals from 401(k), 403(b), regular IRAs, and other tax-deferred accounts are included in the number.

As a result, there may be a significant advantage in withdrawing from your tax-deferred accounts after you retire and before you start collecting Social Security.

You may also want to use up your tax-deferred accounts before you withdraw from your Roth accounts and possibly convert your tax-deferred accounts to Roth IRA holdings after or even before you retire and before you start collecting Social Security.

Social Security's online benefit calculators won't help you much beyond getting a "baseline" idea for what your benefits may be.

When it comes to detailed and/or complex scenarios, strategies, or situations like spousal, divorcee, child, or survivor options, you'll want to work with a financial professional who has the tools needed to help you.

Applying the Earnings Test

While taxes and your Social Security benefits are a point of concern while you are retired, anyone who has filed to receive their Social Security benefit before their Full Retirement Age (particularly while still working or having gone back to work) will face a different kind of taxation. They will have various situations where their benefit will be limited by the Earnings Test.

If you are younger than Full Retirement Age during the full year, Social Security will deduct $1 from your benefits for every $2 you earn above a certain limit ($18,240 in 2020).

If you reach Full Retirement Age during the year, Social Security will deduct $1 from your benefits for every $3 you earn above a certain limit ($48,660 in 2020) until the month you reach full retirement age.

However, you don't lose out permanently.

If you take benefits early and lose some or all of them because of the Earnings Test, those will be tacked back onto your Social Security benefit at your Full Retirement Age, based on the number of months of benefits you forfeited.

This is true whether the loss in benefits, due to the earnings test, reflects benefits based on your own work record or based on your spouse's work record.

If you are under the Full Retirement Age and are collecting a spousal benefit, AND your spouse has not yet attained Full Retirement Age but is collecting a retirement benefit, it is possible your spousal benefit may be reduced if your spouse earns beyond the Earnings Test's exempt amount.

Furthermore, it can also be reduced if YOU earn beyond the Earnings Test's exempt amount.

Getting the Timing Right

No financial advantage exists to deferring the collection of spousal benefits beyond Full Retirement Age, as these don't earn delayed retirement credits.

Equally, no financial advantage exists to deferring the collection of survivor benefits beyond Full Retirement Age.

Up until your Full Retirement Age, there would be a benefit in waiting because you wouldn't face early reduction penalties.

There is no financial advantage to continue to defer credits past age seventy. You can only earn delayed retirement credits up until age seventy.

How Divorce Affects Social Security

If you are divorced *and* your marriage lasted ten years or longer, you can receive benefits on your ex-spouse's record (even if he or she has remarried).

Moreover, if you were born before January 2, 1954, both of you would be able to collect spousal benefits (on the other's work histories), after Full Retirement Age, while still postponing your own retirement benefits until later.

This was an advantage for divorcees. But, for anyone born after January 2, 1954, now if they apply for a spousal benefit, they will automatically be deemed to have applied for all retirement benefits. The Social Security Administration will award them the highest benefit, whether it is their own or their (ex)spousal benefit, but they will not be able to switch later on.

Filing as an ex-spouse is not much different than filing as a spouse, with one notable exception: Someone filing for ex-spousal benefits doesn't have to wait until their ex has filed for their benefits. Additionally, both ex-spouses will *not* receive any notification that their ex has filed, even if they're filing on the other's benefit. This is a different scenario than if you were still married.

Starting Again If You Make the Wrong Choice

Many people aren't aware that, if you started collecting Social Security retirement benefits within the last year and suddenly decide it wasn't the right move, you can repay all the benefits received, including spousal and child benefits, and reapply for potentially higher benefits at a future date.

This maneuver essentially "resets" everything as though it did not happen.

If you decide to wait to collect your Social Security retirement benefit until after you reach your Full Retirement Age (but before you hit age seventy), you will have to wait until the next January to see your full delayed retirement credit show up in your monthly check.

Getting Advice

As you try to work your way through this maze, you'll probably want information and advice.

So, it's important to know the Social Security Administration has provided very specific directions to their employees about offering advice to claimants. In their operations manual for employees, they specifically state the role of the employee is to:

> *"Provide Social Security program information and not attempt to persuade the claimant about benefit decisions."*

They also state the employees "should not provide any advice" concerning the decision. What this means is they are there to answer questions relating to facts about your eligibility, but they are not in a position to strategize with you about what may be the most advantageous time for you and/or your spouse to file for benefits.

This decision is one you need to make and one you should discuss with a professional who is aware of your entire financial picture.

Recent Claiming Changes

There have been important changes recently regarding claiming Social Security, and we have covered these in more detail in Appendix 4: What Every Pre- and Post- Retiree Needs to Know About the Recent Social Security Claiming Changes and What It Means for You!

What We've Learned in This Chapter

• Social Security is beneficial but also complex, so you need to know your entitlements well.

The decision about **when** to take your retirement benefits is crucial.

As well as your own benefits, you need to take spousal benefits into account.

If you start taking your Social Security benefits early, they may be limited, depending on your income (but they will be paid to you later).

Even if you are divorced, you and your former spouse have entitlement to benefits based on each other's work record.

While there is sometimes a benefit in waiting to receive your benefits, there is usually no benefit in waiting too long.

The Social Security Administration can provide information about your entitlements but cannot advise you on the best choices.

Checklist: Choosing the Right Social Security Filing Option

√ Do you know your Social Security entitlements, including those based on your spouse's record?

√ Do you know how the different sources of pension income you hold will be taxed?

√ Have you obtained an estimate of your Social Security benefits?

√ Do you understand your spousal benefits—especially if you have had more than one spouse?

√ Do you know when you want to start taking Social Security benefits?

√ Do you understand the advantages of deferring benefits until a later date?

√ Are you aware of the different strategies available to receive the best combination of benefits between you and your spouse?

√ Do you know where you can find reliable advice about your Social Security benefits and options?

KEY #4

Protecting Your Health and Financial Security for Life

"If I let myself get bitten by a vampire so I become immortal and only a wooden stake can kill me, can I get a better rate on my life insurance?"

Throughout life, we must consider how to protect ourselves and our loved ones against unexpected events, such as a serious illness, disablement, incapacitation, and death.

Sometimes this seems easier when we are younger, and perhaps because we perceive these risks as more theoretical—something that we can plan for but that we can mentally and emotionally dismiss as unlikely to actually happen to us.

In addition, we are more likely to have coverage, such as medical insurance and life insurance, through work.

However, this kind of protection becomes more necessary as we get older and are more likely to need it. For the same reason, it can often be more difficult to receive the protection we need. Because older individuals typically present a higher risk to insurance carriers, this protection can also be somewhat expensive. In any case, protecting the financial security of yourself and your loved ones is a must.

Here's what we're going to cover in this section:

- Key Factors Influencing the Protection of Your Financial Security
- The Ongoing Need for Life Insurance
- Health Insurance in Retirement and Medicare
- Long-Term Care Insurance

So, let's get started on the details of each.

Key Factors Influencing the Protection of Your Financial Security

Here are some factors you need to consider when thinking about how to protect your financial security in retirement:

Family longevity and health record: While you should never make assumptions, it is helpful to consider the health track record within your family.

If people in your family have generally lived for a long time and have been generally healthy, you may reflect on this differently compared to someone with a family history where people have died young or needed major medical care later in life.

Health history of you and your spouse: Equally, your own health record and the record of your spouse are both significant in anticipating future costs.

For example, if you have experienced serious illnesses, this may affect your ability to receive certain insurance. However, it may also help you gain better annuity rates.

Family support available: If you have family living near you and have the time and resources to care for you, this may lead you to make different decisions about long-term care.

Equally, it's advisable not to rely on their ability or willingness to become a caregiver.

Assets available as backup: If you have assets available you can draw on (such as a second home), you may feel this reduces your need for certain financial protection.

But, you can't always rely on being able to sell these assets, and it's easy to underestimate the cost of certain medical care or long-term care.

Social Security record: Being able to rely on Social Security benefits can be important in your time of need.

However, it should typically be regarded as a safety net only, since the benefits are limited and often restrict your choices.

Ongoing liabilities: These days, many people continue debt, such as mortgages and loans, into retirement.

It's important to continue the protection for these as long as that is needed.

Existing insurance coverage: You may be able to benefit from existing insurance coverage after retirement.

For example, some policies will allow you to continue coverage at special rates or with some limited requirements for medical evidence.

Taking these into account, here are some of the issues most often asked about.

The Ongoing Need for Life Insurance

It's tempting to think you'll have less need for life insurance and family protection later in life due to your children having grown up and reached their own independence. Not to mention, many of your big expenses will also likely be behind you, such as buying your main home.

> *You'll continue insurance on your home and car in retirement, so why not your life?*

However, the reality is not so simple. Often, we still have family commitments—not just to a surviving spouse, but also to grandkids or dependent children.

And these days, many people continue some debts into retirement years—either through necessity or choice.

Let's face it, you'll continue insurance on other valuable assets, such as your home and your car. So why wouldn't you want to continue insuring your most important asset: your life?

Of course, your needs will change, and this means you must keep them under review and seek professional advice.

The questions you should ask yourself are the same now as they are at any time in your life. The answers to those questions may just be different than a few years earlier. Some of those questions include:

- What will your family need for the short-term if you die?
- What will your family need in the long-term if you die?
- What are the total resources available to your family right now?
- How much insurance coverage would you need to cover any shortfall?

When you think about short term needs, consider expenses occurring within six months of death, such as loans and credit balances that must be repaid.

You also must consider the expenses arising as a direct result of your death—funeral expenses, medical costs, and estate settlement costs, including taxes (the next chapter will discuss more about estate taxes).

> *The really frightening thing about middle age is that you know you'll grow out of it.*
>
> **Doris Day**

These principles apply whether one of the partners is left alone on death of a spouse or if the family has to make arrangements after the death of the second.

Your surviving spouse and/or dependents should also have an emergency fund with enough funds to help them survive at least six months.

For a surviving spouse, you then need to consider income to cover long-term needs, such as cost of living, elderly care expenses, mortgages, or other loans. It's a good idea to set aside some savings to cover this. While the government provides some programs to help you as well, it's also essential to think about making extra arrangements to cover any shortfall.

Life insurance, one of these extra arrangements, can help cover this shortfall. You pay a premium to an insurance company, and they pay your beneficiaries a specified death benefit when you die.

Life insurance comes in many different forms, and each has its pros and cons. It's important to speak to a skilled financial professional to find advice when deciding the form most suited to your needs.

For example, **term life insurance**:

- Remains the simplest kind of insurance.
- Pays a specific lump sum to whomever you designate.
- Includes the death benefit equal to the policy limit chosen at issue.

As an alternative, **permanent life insurance** (also known as "cash value" life insurance) also includes a savings component.

The cash value of a permanent policy depends on what has been paid into it and the total interest earned. If it is adequately funded, you may be able to skip premium payments or even take loans from it.

This can be a good choice for situations, including a permanent need, such as a husband who wants to provide for his wife.

In addition, remember, insurance is not just about living and dying. You can also have insurance paid out in the event of a serious illness or disability.

Health Insurance in Retirement and Medicare

It's no surprise the cost of medical insurance rises significantly as we age because people tend to have greater needs for health care later on in their lives.

Fortunately, the federal health program, Medicare, kicks in at age sixty-five and helps remove some of these concerns.

Essentially, there are four parts to Medicare, and you need to choose the right options for your situation:

Medicare Part A: Hospital insurance

This covers hospitalization and is free for those who qualify.

Medicare Part B: Medical insurance

This covers doctor visits and outpatient care, and a monthly premium is required.

Medicare Part C: Medicare Advantage

This combines the original Medicare (Parts A and B) with extended services and prescription drug coverage through a private provider for an additional premium.

Medicare Part D: Prescription Drug Coverage

This helps pay for medications prescribed by doctors, and it also requires a monthly premium.

Several choices must be made when it comes to Medicare, and many different costs are involved.

When you combine the various costs, it may end up totaling less than you have been paying for private insurance. Yet, it's beneficial to take these costs into account in planning your budget.

> **It's vital to take the cost of health care insurance into account when planning your retirement budget.**

If you're already receiving Social Security benefits, you are automatically enrolled in Medicare Parts A and B. In fact, to make it easier, the premiums for Part B are deducted from your monthly benefits check.

However, you need to enroll in Part D yourself (if you want it) and choose a plan to receive prescription drug coverage. Similarly, choosing coverage for Part C is your own responsibility.

If you're not yet receiving Social Security benefits, you are still eligible for full Medicare benefits at age sixty-five, but it's up to you to contact the Social Security Administration to sign up.

Remember, while Medicare parts A and B cover a great deal—hospitalization, doctor visits, and essential medical equipment—they don't cover everything.

> How old would you be if you didn't know how old you were?
>
> Satchel Paige

For example, you have to allow for deductibles and copayments.

Bear in mind, also, Medicare is a state-run program, and rules can vary, so a specific medical need covered in one state or county may be denied in another.

This means it can be useful to consider supplemental insurance. Consider the two main types:

Medicare Supplement Policies (also known as Medigap) are sold by private insurance companies, and they pay for things Medicare doesn't cover, such as copayments and deductibles.

These policies generally don't cover prescription drugs, dental, or vision services.

Although Medigap policies are standardized and regulated, costs and coverage can vary.

You must be enrolled in Medicare Parts A and B to qualify for Medicare Supplement insurance.

State Pharmaceutical Assistance Programs (SPAP) plans are offered by some states to help their residents pay for prescription drugs.

Each program works differently and may have different requirements in order to qualify. The states often coordinate their SPAP with Medicare Part D plans.

Realistically, Medicare does not cover all medical expenses. In fact, it is estimated Medicare, on average, only covers between one-half and three-fourths of an enrollee's health care expenses.

> **Medicare was really only intended to help seniors with minor or short-term illnesses.**

What's more, the gap between what Medicare pays and what you are charged is only expected to widen.

Medicare was really only intended to help seniors with minor or short-term illnesses.

If you have a longer-lasting illness—for some, a harsh reality of growing old—you will need to consider more coverage.

We are not talking about a few hundred dollars here. For instance, Medicare may pay nothing for hospital stays longer than ninety days, depending on your total lifetime record. If you remain in the hospital for longer, you could be paying hundreds of dollars a day for your care. Copayments may also cost hundreds of dollars and must come directly out of your pocket.

We cover this in much more detail in Appendix 3: The ABCD of Medicare and How to Avoid the Five Most Common Enrollment Mistakes

For more information on Medicare, take a look at **www.medicare.gov**.

Long-Term Care Insurance

Even though we live longer these days, only a small portion of the population is arranging for long-term care insurance.

One reason is most of us don't like to think about ending up in a nursing home. We usually don't believe it will happen to us—either because we won't live so long, or we don't think we stand at a high risk of needing this type of care.

Perhaps we believe our family or the government will take care of us. But, sadly, many people do end up needing long-term care in a formal setting, and you need to plan for it in case it happens to you. Otherwise, the cost could eat up every dollar you have saved throughout the years.

At the end of the day, long-term care insurance is just like every other kind of insurance—you have to pay for it when you don't need it. Just like you can't get collision insurance for your car right after you've had an accident, you can't get a long-term care policy after you've been diagnosed with the need for it.

The other consideration putting people off long-term care insurance is the expense. However, long-term care itself is also expensive. The cost can amount to tens or even hundreds of thousands of dollars per year. So, you're not just protecting yourself when you plan for long-term care. You are also protecting your children from taking on the costs of nursing home care or having to decide who will take care of you.

> **Most of us don't like to think about ending up in a nursing home.**

When you own long-term care insurance, you decide where you receive your care. Many seniors believe they'll be able to rely on Medicaid if the need for care arises, but, in our opinion, this usually proves to be a mistake.

We believe Medicaid should only be a last resort option, not the option of a prudent person who plans ahead.

Under Medicaid, the government determines where you will be placed for long-term care, so you may end up many miles from your family and friends.

Medicaid also does not provide assistance for long-term care in your own home.

So, let's take a look at what we mean by long-term care.

Long-term care applies to a person who requires someone else to help them with their physical and/or emotional needs over an extended period of time.

This help may be required for many of the activities healthy people take for granted, such as walking, bathing, using the bathroom, and eating.

The need may arise due to a terminal condition, disability, illness, injury, or simply the infirmity of old age.

Of all individuals who live to age sixty-five, 70 percent will need some kind of long-term care.[5]

The need for long-term care may only last for a few weeks or months, or it may continue for years. It all depends on the underlying reasons for needing care.

---

[5] LongTermCare.gov. 2019. "Who Needs Care?" https://longtermcare.acl.gov/the-basics/who-needs-care.html

Before you discuss costs for care, you will need to make some choices regarding:

- Where you will receive care
- The amount of daily benefit the care provides
- The elimination period
- The term of coverage
- A lump sum or annual payment

Naturally, most people prefer to receive care inside their homes. Sometimes this works well. However, it's not always possible. The advantage of completing the financial planning for a potential long-term care need is you will have a choice in the matter.

> We believe Medicaid should only be a last-resort option.

People often either delay or never purchase long-term care coverage because of the cost. However, you do have several options to reduce or avoid the expense.

You might not need the most expensive policy, but at least consider the most basic policy because it is better than none at all.

Case Study: Grace

We met Grace through one of our seminars.

She had previously done her research and decided to purchase a traditional long-term care insurance policy.

She wanted excellent coverage and willingly bought it at the cost of about $5,000 per year.

She is now sixty-five years old and quite healthy.

If she lives for twenty more years, she will pay total premiums of $100,000 during her lifetime.

At one of our first meetings we discussed, because she had longevity in her family and was very healthy now, how it was possible she might never use the insurance.

If she didn't, she would have paid over $100,000 in premiums and received zero LTC benefits!

> **If she never used the insurance, she would have paid over $100,000 in premiums and received zero LTC benefits.**

Despite doing her research, she had never considered this fact.

We prefer, when possible, to use a policy called Asset-Based Long-Term Care Protection (ABLTC).

This links the benefits of life insurance and long-term care (a policy feature, called a rider, available at an additional cost) into a single policy where the policyholder can draw out of the bucket meeting their most urgent need.

What We've Learned in This Chapter

Financial protection is just as important in retirement as at any other stage in life.

We need to provide for the immediate needs, as well as the long-term needs, of our family after death.

You and your spouse may benefit from each other's Social Security contribution record.

Many different types of life insurance suit a range of scenarios.

The health insurance options in retirement are complicated, and we need to be aware of the different alternatives.

Many of the Medicare benefits are limited, and we may need supplementary coverage.

We may not be able to rely on Medicare and Medicaid if something serious happens to our health.

Checklist: Protecting Your Health and Financial Security

√ Do you *really* know what supports your family could provide for you if something serious happened to your health?

√ Do you understand the limits of Medicare and Medicaid?

√ Have you budgeted for the extra costs of health care insurance in retirement?

√ Do you know how your spouse will be financially affected if anything happens to you?

√ Do you realize how much it would cost if you had to receive long-term care?

√ Do you know the options available for covering the costs of long-term care?

KEY #5

Passing Wealth on to the Next Generation

"It's wonderful that you were able to take it with you. Now what do you plan to do with it?"

CartoonStock.com

One of the biggest misconceptions we observe in financial planning is this myth: Estate planning only applies to "wealthy" people.

This results in considerable financial—and emotional—grief to many American families of all income and asset levels.

The IRS collects over twenty-six billion dollars in estate taxes every year, and many of these likely come from families whose parents did nothing to avoid or eliminate the taxes due.[6]

Planning for your finances after your death provides for a number of different elements, including:

- Ensuring your assets transfer to whomever you decide.
- Avoiding family confusion and squabbles.
- Keeping your money out of the hands of the government as much as legally possible.
- Contributing to your favorite charities.
- Taking care of your children and grandchildren in the way you choose, e.g., protecting their education.

At its simplest, estate planning means making sure you can leave your money and property to the right people while avoiding confusion and minimizing the amount of taxes they will have to pay to receive those benefits.

Key Factors Influencing Your Estate Planning

Here are some of the factors you need to consider when you think about estate planning:

Amount of wealth: You don't need to be very wealthy to think about estate planning, but the more wealth you have, the more essential this type of planning becomes.

---

[6] Chye-Ching Huang and Chloe Cho. Center on Budget and Policy Priorities. October 30, 2017. "Ten Facts You Should Know About the Federal Estate Tax." https://www.cbpp.org/research/federal-tax/ten-facts-you-should-know-about-the-federal-estate-tax

Remember, your wealth includes many elements, and you are probably worth more than you think.

Family circumstances: The more complicated your family circumstances, the more important it is to be clear about what you want to happen.

For example, if your history includes divorce or children with different parents, the situation can get complicated.

Tax situation: Planning for retirement must take into account all aspects of your tax situation.

Most people want to minimize taxes at all stages, not just after they die.

Chosen heirs: Do you have specific people you want your assets to be passed to?

For example, you may want your house to go to a specific person but your business to someone else.

Ownership of assets: An important factor to consider is who legally owns your assets.

For example, they may be jointly owned with your spouse or held in a trust.

Assets passed during lifetime: Many people want to pass assets on to family during their lifetime.

It's important to plan this in advance so beneficiaries do not face huge costs later.

Life insurance: Life insurance can play a valuable role in estate planning.

There are many ways to use it to help minimize the impact of taxes on your chosen heirs.

Taking these elements into account, here are some of the key factors we will consider:

• Steps for Creating an Estate Plan
• Passing Assets on to Family During Your Lifetime
• The Role of Life Insurance in Estate Planning
• What Happens If You Are Unable to Make Decisions in Later Life

Steps for Creating an Estate Plan

The steps for creating an estate plan are very important and can change at any given time.

Therefore, it's important to make sure you receive the right advice from qualified professionals.

> **If you die without leaving a will, the government effectively dictates what happens to your assets and property.**

Following are some of the key steps to consider.

Get a Will

The majority of Americans die without leaving a will.

This means, in reality, the government dictates what happens to their assets and property.

This can mean assets end up passing on to an estranged spouse or to out-of-favor relatives.

Whether or not there is a surviving spouse, most people have clear preferences about the people and/or entities they want to provide for after their death.

Writing a will is the best way to ensure this happens. It also avoids confusion and disagreements among the family.

Plan for Probate

Although a will provides a good beginning, probate is still required when assets are only registered in the name of the person who has died.

This means your house, your bank account, or your car may be subjected to a lengthy, costly, and public process after your death to determine who takes over them.

The most common way to avoid probate is by:

- Using trusts
- Designating beneficiaries on retirement accounts and insurance policies
- Setting up debt accounts
- Titling property as joint

If taxes will be an issue for you, it may be advisable to use a combination of trusts to direct more of your estate toward your intended beneficiaries.

Passing Assets on to Family During Lifetime

Many people experience great satisfaction in giving some of their assets to family or charities while they are still alive.

Each year, you can gift a certain amount to as many individuals as you like, tax-free. Doing so can help to reduce the overall size of your estate, reducing, in turn, the amount of tax due.

The Role of Life Insurance in Estate Planning

Ben Franklin famously said, "Nothing in this world is certain but death and taxes."

So far, nobody has discovered a solution to remove the certainty of death, but we can use many ways to ensure tax is not so inevitable.

Even if it can't be completely removed, we can take several steps to help minimize taxes due upon death.

If you have enough wealth to expect your estate will be taxed, life insurance in a trust is one of the strategies you can use to help minimize this burden.

While the estate tax exclusion at the federal level is more than $11.5 million per person (in 2020), the variations at the state level may cut in at a lower amount.[7]

So, if estate taxes may be due in the event of your or your spouse's death, it is worth seeking advice about your options for reducing them.

A common approach is to use a universal life or whole life insurance policy to provide your family with the funds needed to pay estate taxes.

> Fun is like life insurance; the older you get, the more it costs.
>
> Kin Hubbard

This can be done through an irrevocable life insurance trust (ILIT), which offers a variety of benefits.

One of the main reasons people set up an ILIT is to help provide their heirs with flexibility in settling the estate.

The top federal tax rate in 2020 is 37 percent, and many states impose additional estate and inheritance taxes. Heirs may face the problem of not having access to cash to pay this when it is

---

[7] Ashlea Ebeling. *Forbes.* November 6, 2019. "IRS Announces Higher Estate And Gift Tax Limits For 2020." https://www.forbes.com/sites/ashleaebeling/2019/11/06/irs-announces-higher-estate-and-gift-tax-limits-for-2020/#3addd6c92efb

due. (We provide information on the Tax Cuts and Jobs Act of 2017 in Appendix 5 at the back of this book).

This can mean they are then forced to sell real estate, stocks, or a family business to raise the necessary cash. But, there can be a number of problems when doing so:

- First, it may not be convenient to do this before the end of the nine-month period when estate taxes are due.
- Second, your heirs may want to keep the assets such as your home, jewelry, or art rather than sell them.
- Third, you can't choose the timing, so if the forced sale coincides with a poor stock market or depressed real estate values, it is not the ideal time to sell, and the returns will be diminished.
- Finally, there is also the risk selling could trigger additional income or capital gains taxes.

A key advantage of an ILIT is if the trust is set up and administered correctly, the assets owned by the ILIT will not be considered part of your estate for inheritance/estate tax purposes.

This means your heirs won't have to pay estate or inheritance taxes on them.

The premiums on the life insurance policy are paid by the trust, which means the grantor must transfer sufficient money into the trust or pay directly on behalf of the trust to cover them.

Insurance helps because an ILIT uses gifts made to the trust to pay for insurance premiums.

These gifts are removed from the estate, and the benefits paid out to your heirs will not be included as part of your estate for tax purposes.

A major potential advantage of an ILIT—and of life insurance in general—is a death benefit is not considered taxable income by the IRS.

> **The avoidance of taxes is the only intellectual pursuit that still carries any reward.**
>
> John Maynard Keynes

However, while there are potential tax advantages of an ILIT, it is not an automatic choice.

Setting up a trust requires a complex legal arrangement whose creation demands professional assistance, and this is best done before starting the insurance plan.

As the name "irrevocable" suggests, once it is set up, you cannot terminate it, make changes to it, or withdraw the assets you've put into it.

If a couple sets up the trust jointly, the policy is usually a "survivorship" or second-to-die policy, so the death benefit isn't paid until both spouses pass away.

When the person who sets up the trust (or the surviving spouse) dies, the proceeds from the insurance policy flow into the trust and are eventually distributed to the trust beneficiaries—often children, grandchildren, or other family members of the person who set it up. You also need to qualify for the policy through underwriting, and, as noted above, you need to be able to properly fund it throughout your lifetime.

These trusts are not suitable for everyone, but they can be extremely valuable in appropriate cases.

What Happens If You Are Unable to Make Decisions in Later Life?

It's a good idea to set up legal documentation to let your doctors and family know how you wish to be treated in the case of an emergency or near the end of your life.

It's something no one wants to think about, but it's equally not something you want to leave to your relatives when you are no longer able to deal with the situation.

An Advanced Health Care Directive and a Durable Power of Attorney will provide clear instructions, as well as nominate a specific person to have authority to act on your behalf.

Case Study: Miriam

Miriam was a sixty-eight-year-old woman.

She had some health issues, and family circumstances determined she became the major caretaker for her great-niece.

At the time, she had several hundred thousand dollars in savings, and her only form of income was Social Security and income from an IRA.

Her most pressing goal was to leave a legacy for her great-niece by paying for her college.

One option Miriam could consider would be life insurance. This often doesn't occur to people because, like Miriam, they think of life insurance as "blood money" instead of as a viable financial tool.

While there are many options for how someone can fund an ex-

pense like college, with life insurance, they could either pay ongoing premiums or transfer assets as a lump sum into a single premium policy. Either way, the leveraged premium dollars today would help fund the anticipated bill in the future, be received tax-free by the beneficiary, and could be paid out into a trust, if preferred.

(Note: If someone purchases life insurance early on and accumulates "paid-up" life insurance policies over the years, it may be feasible to exchange the existing cash values for a new, "more cost-efficient" policy with larger "paid-up" death benefits using no additional premiums. There is a caution with this strategy: It is important to consider whether there are costs, risks, fees, or penalties—including the implementation of a new surrender period—associated with doing so.)

What We've Learned in This Chapter

Estate planning is not just for the very rich.

Many Americans die without leaving a will.

Making your wishes clear in advance helps avoid family arguments and additional costs.

Taking the right steps now can prevent the government from laying its hands on more of your money.

Life insurance can play an important role in estate planning.

Taking action now will provide for not being able to make your own decisions later in life.

You can take steps to avoid the costs and delays of probate.

Checklist: Passing Wealth on to the Next Generation

√ Do you know how you want your assets to be distributed after your death?

√ Have you taken steps to record those desires?

√ Do you know what the expectations of your family are, and could these cause any problems?

√ Do you have complications in your estate planning, such as previous spouses or children from previous marriages?

√ Do you have any assets in trust?

√ Do you have any life insurance policies in place, and are they properly set up to maximize the tax benefits?

Appendices

APPENDIX 1

Nine Retirement Mistakes to Avoid

One of the best ways to ensure you have the retirement you want is to take steps to avoid the key mistakes many people make.

An article in 2017 by Martin McCann laid out a list of the top nine retirement mistakes people could avoid. Though we like a few of the key mistakes McCann offers, we have added some points of our own and changed the order around. Here we list what we feel rank as some of the most common we see in our office. [8]

MISTAKE 1: Leaving 401(k) money with an old employer

This can be problematic because you run the risk of losing control of your money.

Your employer's "plan document" dictates where your money goes, and the old plan you had may not allow you to control investment providers and investment options. You are left at its mercy.

---

[8] Martin McCann. McCann Asset Management. May 12, 2017. "Nine 401(k) Mistakes to Avoid." https://www.mccannam.com/blog/nine-401k-mistakes-to-avoid

Another problem is, if you pass away, your beneficiaries may not even realize you own the account since people often forget about old plans.[9]

MISTAKE 2: Executing a rollover instead of doing a direct transfer

If you've elected to move your 401(k) over to an IRA, you have only two options concerning how you move the money.

With the rollover option, you can instruct your current 401(k) plan provider to send you a check (payable to you), and you can then send your new IRA provider the money. But, there's a catch. You only have sixty days to reinvest the money before you incur taxes on the entire amount.

Not only could missing the sixty-day window cost you in taxes, but this option also requires your current 401(k) provider to withhold tax on the distribution made to you. Thus, you will receive only about 80 percent of the original value.

Finally, you're only allowed to make this type of transaction once over every twelve-month span.

A second, better option to consider is executing a direct transfer. In order to execute a direct transfer, you simply tell your 401(k) provider to send a check directly to the new IRA provider.

This eliminates the risk of missing the sixty-day window, avoiding that surprise 1099 in the mail, and is so much simpler and cleaner.

This option may require specific paperwork, and, unfortunately, some employers may only offer the first option—making the check payable to you.

---

[9] Ibid.

In this case, it is best to have them write the check to your new financial institution to avoid the 20 percent withholding.[10]

MISTAKE 3: Failing to properly name beneficiaries

This seems like common sense, but it still remains a common mistake we see with people who first visit our office.

Your 401(k) and IRA are passed to whoever is on your beneficiary form accompanying the account. This designation trumps any will, trust, or other estate plans you may have.

Life is full of changes. Marriages happen and are dissolved, kids are born and adopted, and those we care for pass away. It's essential to ensure your retirement accounts reflect those changes in who they name as beneficiaries. Be sure you check and re-check those forms often.

Many people think the idea of leaving money to an already established trust account could make the whole process easier. While seemingly logical, doing this can eliminate certain tax advantages for beneficiaries, which could significantly diminish their overall returns.

Also, starting in January 2020, who you name as the beneficiary of your traditional IRA and other traditional retirement plans can make a significant difference in how that money is taxed if it is someone other than a spouse. That is because the SECURE Act, which took effect January 1, 2020, eliminated the "stretch" IRA, with a few exceptions, such as for spouses, beneficiaries fewer than ten years younger, and disabled children.

A stretch IRA strategy was oftentimes used in the past to help ease the burden of taxation all at once by "stretching" the inherited IRA distributions through a beneficiary's life, based on their longer life expectancy.

---

[10] Ibid.

Using a stretch IRA allowed the account owner to continue deferring taxes on the growth of those IRA funds, so, even though the distributions would be taxed as they were withdrawn, the beneficiary could keep more funds in the account, growing and compounding.

This stretch strategy is no longer an option for anyone who inherited an IRA after January 1, 2020. By eliminating the stretch IRA, non-spousal beneficiaries are now required to withdraw all of the funds within ten years of the initial account holder's death. (These rules also apply to inherited 401(k)s, regardless of whether they are rolled into a traditional or Roth IRA.)

This means, although there is no annual minimum withdrawal requirement, no RMD, the entire balance of the inherited IRA account must be distributed by the end of the tenth year after the original account holder's death, period.

Placing a time limit on the account's distributions can possibly increase the tax burden to the recipient. These rules might be especially cumbersome for beneficiaries who are in their forties or fifties, and who are often in the peak of their earning years and consequently in higher income tax brackets.

Consider the case of any minors, too. Different states hold certain limits on the amount of money they allow minors to control, which may affect how you allocate your funds.[11]

MISTAKE 4: Trying to recoup losses or chase performance

We all know the stock market moves both up and down.

Perhaps you move your 401(k) during a market slump. Your human nature may suggest making an effort to quickly recover your losses by investing more heavily in the market.

---

[11] Ibid.

Be careful. Don't let the emotion of the loss veer you off course from your financial plan and long-term vision.

Conservative investments are much more ideal than aggressive ones as you near retirement, and you must remember you need your money to last for decades. [12]

MISTAKE 5: Underestimating the importance of your Social Security benefits

Many people pay too little attention to Social Security in retirement planning. The truth is, for many retirees, Social Security will become a key part of their retirement income.

You need to understand how to make the most of your Social Security benefits during retirement, as this selection could last for roughly a third of your life.

Like most new retirees, you have probably been paying into Social Security far longer than you have contributed to your defined contribution plans.

You must consider both as critical sources of income.

MISTAKE 6: Rushing to collect Social Security benefits

While you can begin collecting Social Security benefits as early as age sixty-two, you may not want to.

The big downside to collecting early is your benefits will be reduced by 25 percent for life.

To receive your full payment, you should wait until you reach Full Retirement Age (if you can afford it), which is currently sixty-six for anyone born between 1943 and 1954.

---

[12] Ibid.

For those born between 1955 and 1959, the full retirement age for Social Security gradually rises toward sixty-seven, and, from 1960 on, FRA rests at sixty-seven.

MISTAKE 7: Not understanding how married couples can integrate their Social Security benefits.

If you're married, you can either take a Social Security benefit based on your work history or half of your spouse's benefit.

So, if you earned more than your spouse did, and you have a higher benefit as a result, compare and discover which will pay the most.

Social Security benefits can also be claimed based on an ex-spouse's work record if you were married for at least ten years.

MISTAKE 8: Not planning ahead for taxes

Depending on the sum of your adjusted gross income, nontaxable interest, and your Social Security benefits, up to 85 percent of your Social Security benefits may be taxable.

You can minimize this expense by using certain tax-saving moves, such as purchasing an annuity.

MISTAKE 9: Not doing your due diligence for Social Security benefits

You should always read your Social Security statements (either received as paper statements in the mail or online at SocialSecurity.gov/mystatement) to be sure everything has been reported correctly.

Although inaccuracies are uncommon, some scenarios lend themselves to a greater chance of error.

APPENDIX 2:

Milestones for the Retirement Lifestyle You Want

One of the most significant challenges for most people is they don't really have a clear picture of where they currently stand.

Although many people might have some idea of what's in their bank account and how much they owe on their credit cards, they can't really put their finger on the exact details. So, the first step toward a better retirement is getting clear about where you currently stand.

It's crucial to take time to undergo this exercise to work out your current financial position.

Part of this means working out what's called your "net worth." Net worth is the difference between your assets and your liabilities; what you own minus what you owe.

In summation:

- An **asset** is something you own.
- A **liability** is something you owe.

Your net worth is, therefore, the difference between what you own and what you owe.

Actually taking the time to write down these numbers in relation to your finances is key in crafting a financial strategy.

Unfortunately, people often think they are well off because they live in an expensive house, but they forget to take into account the huge mortgage balance they may still owe. What's worse is, sometimes—like in the recession of 2008—the value of many peoples' homes drops. In the past, some have even dropped to a much lower value than what they owed on their mortgage.

When it comes to determining net worth, people also may not fully realize the value of the assets they have built up.

That's why it's essential to take time to work out where you are on your journey to your ideal retirement.

To help you do that, we're going to take you through a series of milestones on the journey.

We call these the Retirement Ready milestones:

- Knowing Your Current Net Worth
- Knowing Where Your Money Goes Now
- Envisioning Your Retirement
- Knowing What You'll Need in Retirement

Retirement Ready Milestone #1: Knowing Your Current Net Worth

Now it's time to gather all your financial information in one place and collate it.

If you've never done this process before, and you don't keep very good financial records, you may find this a bit painful. But it will be a real eye-opener for you. Additionally, doing this now will make it easier to track your financial standing moving forward.

First, you will need to collect all your financial information from the past twelve months, such as:

- Bank statements
- Credit card bills
- Mortgage and loan statements
- Investment statements

At this stage, the process is all about uncovering an accurate picture of where you are.

The exercise, therefore, is to use the chart that follows and list your assets and liabilities as comprehensively as you can. In some cases, you may have records, but in others you may have to guesstimate.

Start by listing out all your assets irrespective of whether they have loans attached to them. You need to list everything of significance you own. You might start by listing the highest value first and then listing each item in order thereafter.

Assets could include:

- Bank accounts: Checking accounts, savings accounts, money market accounts, and certificate of deposits
- Main home value
- Other property, including any rental and/or vacation homes
- Automobiles: How many, what kind, and estimated worth
- Stocks, bonds, and mutual funds
- 401(k)s, IRAs, Annuities, and other accounts set aside for your future
- Jewelry, artwork, collections, etc.: You probably need this done anyway for insurance purposes. It is best to have these items appraised professionally and to keep the appraisal in a safe place
- Sporting goods such as boats, valuable fishing equipment, or golf clubs

Add the numbers for these assets to the second column.

Wealth-building assets

When you categorize your assets and measure your net worth, it's a good idea to split your assets into wealth-building assets and other assets.

A wealth-building asset is something you own paid to you as income or growing in value with the intention that you can sell it and capture the value in the future. Clear examples of wealth-building assets would be shares of stock, art, or investment property.

Conversely, other assets would include the current market value of your car, as this reduces in value. We also count your main home under "other assets"; although it increases in value, you cannot generally realize its value while living in it.

Liabilities

Next, add up your liabilities. These could include:

- Mortgage
- Car loans
- Credit card balances
- Loans for various things like boats, college, medical services, etc.
- Anything you pay to anyone

Add your liabilities to the third column.

Net Worth

The difference between assets and liabilities provides you with your snapshot of total net worth.

This may take you a while to do, but the time invested will be worth it. By doing this exercise accurately, you will have better success with realistic goal setting.

Your Details

	Assets ($)	Liabilities ($)
Wealth Building Assets		
Bank accounts		
Stocks, bonds, and mutual funds		
401(k)s, IRAs, Annuities		
Jewelry, artwork, and other valuables		
Cash		
Rental property		
Other Assets		
Home		
Car		
Boat		
Liabilities		
Mortgage		
Credit card balances		
Other loans		
Other liabilities		
Total		
Total Assets — Total Liabilities = NET WORTH		

Retirement Ready Milestone #2: Knowing Where Your Money Goes Now

Often the starting point to understanding what you'll need in retirement is knowing what you spend money on now.

Many people have the idea they'll need a lot less money in retirement, but often this isn't the case. So, the next exercise works out your annual budget—the things you spend money on now.

Your outgoings are usually split into regular monthly costs and costs you have to meet less often (perhaps quarterly or annually). In the chart that follows, list your regular outgoings.

Your Details

Monthly Outgoings		Irregular Outgoings	
Description	($)	Description	($)
Monthly x 12		**Annual Total:** (Monthly x 12 + Total Irregular Outgoings)	

Retirement Ready Milestone #3: Envisioning Your Retirement

The next step in the process requires envisioning your future retirement.

- What do you imagine your retirement looks like?
- What do you do during the day?
- Where do you live?
- How do you spend your time and your money?
- What are your passions, interests, and hobbies?
- What does your home look like, and who are you living with?

Whether you draw or write, create your vision for your ideal retirement in the following space.

Create Your Vision for Your Ideal Retirement

Retirement Ready Milestone #4:
Knowing What You'll Need in Retirement

Now that you've done this, look again at your budget from Milestone #2 and determine how your expenditures will change. This offers you an idea of how much you will need in retirement.

Your Details

Monthly Outgoings		Irregular Outgoings	
Description	($)	Description	($)
Monthly x 12		**Annual Total:** (Monthly x 12 + Total Irregular Outgoings)	

Checklist:
Achieving the Retirement Lifestyle You Want

√ Do you know the value of your current assets?

√ Do you know how much you will receive from your current pension plans?

√ Do you know how much money you will need as income in retirement?

√ Do you know what lump sum you will need to build up in order to achieve this income?

√ Do you know what access you might need to your investment assets before retirement—e.g., for college fees, etc.?

√ Have you thought about the lifestyle you might want in retirement and what that will cost?

√ Is there someone you can seek out for reliable financial advice?

APPENDIX 3

The ABCD of Medicare and How to Avoid the Five Most Common Enrollment Mistakes

By Christopher Reyes

It's both surprising and troubling how many financial advisors, in my experience, do not provide their clients with the basic information and planning necessary to navigate one of the most significant concerns pre- and post-retirees have: how they will maintain quality health coverage in retirement.

Fewer and fewer companies are offering retiree benefit programs today. Of the ones who do, the retiree often may have to cover a significant amount of the costs. [13]

Therefore, being proactively made aware of what you need to do when you first become eligible for Medicare remains vital.

Many people are aware age sixty-five marks the magic number when it comes to Medicare eligibility; however, waiting until

---

[13] Frank McArdle, Tricia Neuman, and Jennifer Huang. Kaiser Family Foundation. April 14, 2014. "Retiree Health Benefits at the Crossroads." https://www.kff.org/report-section/retiree-health-benefits-at-the-crossroads-overview-of-health-benefits-for-pre-65-and-medicare-eligible-retirees/

you have a piece of the milestone birthday cake before you enroll could cause some severe enrollment headaches.

Most people do not realize there are several parts to Medicare, and different enrollment periods exist, so Medicare beneficiaries need to make sure they can enroll when they should. You may have a friend or co-worker who missed their enrollment window or still pays a late enrollment penalty.

For many of our clients, a key problem they face is the lack of personalized information available. There is a lot of information available *generally*—too much, even—but not much to filter it to the individual level. It is crucial to know how any changes to Medicare will directly impact a person's immediate situation and whether they will lose any benefits.

Gerald Ford once said, "A government big enough to give you everything you want is a government big enough to take from you everything you have." People in retirement do not want to lose any benefits, but receiving the correct information in order to know your rights and entitlements can prove difficult.

Where to Go for Help . . . Is There Anybody Out There?

The Social Security Administration (SSA), which enrolls retirees into Original Medicare, is not permitted to disclose advice on how to handle the Medicare portion of retirement.

Then how do you know what to do? Isn't this always the million-dollar question? "What must I do to make sure I am making the best choices for myself in the event I need major medical attention?"

Sounds like an easy question; however, it may not always have an easy answer.

The first thing anyone should do is review the "Medicare and You Guide" the Social Security Administration sends out each year to all Medicare beneficiaries.

This guide (though large and cumbersome) contains the current rules and information all in one place. Sometimes, interpreting the literature tends to be a bit tricky, and some explanations may not seem clear at first. Consequently, you may end up having more questions than answers with this option. Let us help!

Simple Explanations of the Four Parts of Medicare:

There are four parts to Medicare, and each part covers a different service.

This is what we call the "ABCD of Medicare:"

Original Medicare is provided directly by the federal government and overseen by the Centers for Medicare and Medicaid Services (CMS).

Original Medicare is composed of:

Part A (Hospital), which covers most medically necessary inpatient hospital services, some skilled nursing care, some home health care, and hospice care.

If you have worked and paid into the Social Security system for forty non-consecutive quarters or ten non-consecutive years, there is *no* charge for Medicare Part A. If you have not paid enough into the system, in 2020, the Medicare Part A cost is $458 per month.

Part B (Medical) covers most medically necessary doctor services, outpatient hospital services, durable medical equipment, laboratory tests, X-rays, and mental health care.

You *will* pay a monthly premium for Part B taken directly out of your social security deposit or billed directly to you quarterly if you are not taking Social Security retirement payments.

In 2020, the monthly Part B premium is $144.60 for most people. However, if you are considered a higher income earner, this premium could be quite a bit more. Also, CMS may change the premium amount each year, if needed.

Medicare Part C & D are optional plans Medicare beneficiaries can enroll in to help cover what Medicare Parts A & B do not cover.

Medicare Part C (Medicare Advantage Plans) are Medicare plans where private insurance companies offer health plans such as HMOs and PPOs.

Medicare Part C can be thought of as an alternative way to receive your Medicare Part A and B benefits. Medicare Advantage plans must include all the benefits of Medicare Part A & B, and some plans include the benefit of Medicare Part D (Prescription Drug Plan) as well.

These plans may also offer additional services, such as dental, vision, and/or hearing aid benefits.

You will be responsible for the costs of your Medicare Advantage plan, which may include deductibles, copays, and/or coinsurance.

There may also be an additional premium you pay for this coverage in addition to your Medicare Part B premium.

Medicare Part D (Prescription Drug Plans) are stand-alone Rx plans you can enroll in. These plans work in conjunction with Original Medicare Parts A & B and/or a Medicare Supplement policy (also known as Medigap Plans).

You will have to pay a premium for Medicare Part D plans in addition to deductibles, copays, and/or coinsurance, depending on the plan design.

Medicare Supplement Policies (also known as Medigap) are private insurance policies you can purchase to cover services Medicare A & B do not cover. For instance, many Medicare Supplement plans will pick up some, or all, of the cost of Medicare Part A & B deductibles, copayments, or coinsurance.

There are ten standardized plans (Plans A through N) offering a range of benefit levels and varying premiums. This plan type does not include prescription drug coverage, and, if you want those benefits, you will also have to enroll in a Medicare Part D (Prescription Drug Plan).

State Pharmaceutical Assistance Programs (SPAP) are programs offered by some states to help their residents pay for prescription drugs. Each program works differently and may have different requirements in order to qualify. The states often coordinate their SPAP with Medicare Part D plans.

If you are currently covered, or soon to be on Medicare, and you want to know if you can qualify for one of these programs, feel free to call or email us at info@retire-usa.com.

Four Enrollment Periods

Now you know the ABCD of Medicare, you will also need to keep these four enrollment periods in mind when your time to enroll rolls around.

Initial Enrollment Period (IEP)

The Center for Medicare and Medicaid Services (CMS) runs the Medicare program for the Federal Government, and they determine the enrollment and eligibility rules.

The IEP refers to the time you first become eligible for Medicare Part A (Hospital) and Part B (Medical). Only a seven-month window exists in which to apply.

The seven months include the month in which you turn sixty-five (or become eligible for Medicare due to disability), the three months prior to your birth month, and the three months following your birth month.

This window is also used for eligibility to enroll in Medicare Part C (Medicare Advantage) and Medicare Part D (Prescription Drug Plan).

If you miss this enrollment period, there is also the option of General Enrollment for Original Medicare from January 1st to March 31st of each year for a July 1st effective date.

However, you may still be charged a lifetime late enrollment penalty on your Part B premium if you enroll in Medicare late.

Open Enrollment (Guarantee Issue)

If you choose to enroll in a Medicare Supplement plan (also called Medigap) to cover what Medicare does not, you need to be aware of a separate six-month enrollment period.

This six-month period begins in your birth month and continues through the five subsequent months.

In this timeframe, you can enroll in a Medicare Supplement plan with *no* medical questions asked.

It can prove extremely beneficial to enroll for a Medicare Supplement plan during this time, as you cannot be turned down for coverage or even charged a higher amount of premium due to an adverse health condition. (This, however, is not the case if you enroll after your initial enrollment period.)

You only have *one* "open enrollment" opportunity for a Medicare Supplement plan.

After your six-month window, the insurance carriers have the right to ask you to complete a medical questionnaire and, consequently, increase your premium should you have current health conditions.

You can also be *denied* coverage altogether after your six-month open enrollment.

Keep in mind, you *cannot* enroll in both a Medicare Advantage Plan *and* a Medicare Supplement plan.

Annual Election Period (AEP)

If you already have a Medicare Part C (Medicare Advantage) or Medicare Part D (Prescription Drug Plan), you are able to switch plans during this Annual Election Period. This fifty-three-day period runs from October 15 to December 7 of each year.

Look into your options early, as you may need to wait a full year to change plans if you miss this window. You are also allowed to drop a Medicare Advantage plan and return to Original Medicare Parts A & B during this time.

A Medicare Advantage Disenrollment Period (MADP) also exists, and it runs from January 1 to February 14 each year.

You can *only* drop a Medicare Advantage Plan and enroll in a Prescription Drug Plan at this time.

Special Election Period (SEP)

Most people cannot make changes outside of the Annual Election Period unless they qualify for a special circumstance.

Some common reasons for a Special Election Period involve cases when you:

- Retiring and losing employer coverage
- Moving out of the plan service area
- Receiving assistance from the State in which you live
- Being or have been diagnosed with certain qualifying disabilities or chronic health conditions

Watch Your Step! The Five Most Common Medicare Enrollment Mistakes We See Happen Explained...

We have detailed the ABCD of Medicare along with the most important enrollment periods every Medicare beneficiary should know, and now it's important to know these five common Medicare enrollment mistakes and understand how to avoid them.

1. Picking the same plan as your spouse, sibling, friend, or neighbor.

Just as everyone's medical needs in retirement are different, the types of Medicare plans available are different, as well.

A plan that is a good fit for your spouse or family member may not provide you with the level of benefit required to obtain quality care.

Some plans may include doctor copays, while others do not. Some plan types require you to use a specific set of in-network contracted physicians, while others allow you to see any doctor accepting Medicare.

Lastly, each plan determines what prescriptions it includes in its drug formulary. So, determining what type of plan you need in conjunction with Original Medicare Parts A and B is highly personal and needs to be cross-referenced with the doctors, hospitals, prescriptions, and types of service you will personally need.

2. Not looking into your options when you are first eligible.

Some people are unaware of the basic Medicare enrollment periods. You *cannot* just enroll whenever you want to! You must follow and understand the previously addressed enrollment periods.

For example, in case you are not aware, once you have enrolled in Medicare Part B, you have a six-month window to enroll in a Medicare Supplement Policy without any medical questions or underwriting required, even if you have pre-existing conditions.

If you enroll after the window, the carriers then have the ability to medically underwrite your policy, which may result in increased premiums or a denial of the policy enrollment.

This could leave someone exposed to significant health care costs and could dramatically impact their retirement nest egg and lifestyle.

This is only one example, as there are several Medicare enrollment and eligibility rules and requirements.

3. Not signing up for Medicare Part B when you have retiree or COBRA coverage.

When you are eligible for Medicare, you enter the world of primary and secondary payers. While you are employed and enrolled in your company plan (assuming your company staffs more than twenty employees), your company plan is the primary payer and Medicare becomes the secondary.

In most circumstances, if you are still covered under an employer-sponsored health plan, you do not need to enroll in Medicare Part B, only Medicare Part A.

When you retire or enroll in COBRA, Medicare becomes your primary payer and the company-sponsored retiree or COBRA plan is your secondary payer.

In this scenario, you *must* have Medicare Part B. If you do not, then your medical claims won't be covered by Medicare, and, by virtue of the primary payer not covering your bills, the secondary payer will deny them as well.

4. Missing the Part B enrollment period after leaving a job or retiring.

Upon termination of employment, you must enroll in Medicare Part B within an eight-month period. This is because, while you are working (age sixty-five or older), as long as you have a company-sponsored plan and are gainfully employed, you need only enroll in Medicare Part A.

Once you leave your job, it gets tricky.

If you miss the Medicare Part B enrollment deadline, you may not only have to wait until January of the following year to enroll, but you may not have effective coverage until July of the next year.

In addition to this, not only may there be a gap in coverage, but you may also face a 10 percent lifetime late-enrollment penalty, which can make your Medicare Part B premiums higher for life.

5. Ignoring Income Thresholds that may affect your Medicare Part B and D premiums.

Most people pay the standard Medicare Part B fee of $144.60 per month in 2020.

However, this could increase if your adjusted gross income reaches $85,000 per year or more (for someone filing an individual tax return), or $170,000 or more for married taxpayers filing jointly.

In fact, four thresholds exist, and each one has a higher premium adjustment than the previous.

This could potentially increase your Medicare Part B premium by more than double the standard rate.

This is also true for Medicare Part D Prescription Drug Plans. In this case, however, the Medicare Part D premium could increase as much as three to four times the premium, depending on what plan you enrolled in.

This is why planning out all your income sources in retirement and coordinating them with your entitlement programs like Social Security and Medicare is vital to winning the retirement game!

The rules to Medicare often change and, with recent years of health care reform, it has never been more important to know your rights and entitlements.

As a bonus to this book, you can request a free breakdown of the plan options in your area, as well as additional information regarding the details provided in this book. Just send an email to info@retire-usa.com.

We can also make sure you have everything accounted for when making the transition into the Medicare program.

APPENDIX 4

What Every Pre- and Post-Retiree Needs to Know About the Recent Social Security Claiming Changes and What They Mean for You!

Now more than ever before, people need to be proactively made aware of changes that may negatively impact their financial situation.

In addition, a plan of action also needs to be put in place to eliminate or mitigate any potential concerns that may arise from changes in economic policy.

What Has Changed?

On November 2, 2015, President Obama signed into law The Bipartisan Budget Act of 2015 (Public Law 114-74). Title VII in the new law addresses changes to the Social Security Disability Program.

The Disability Insurance (DI) Trust Fund was slated to run out of money toward the end of 2016.

In order to keep the program afloat, the new law shifts approximately $150 billion from the traditional Social Security Trust Fund over to the DI Trust Fund.

This will provide funding to the DI Trust Fund until about 2022, when more reform may be needed.

Although the name of the act referencing the federal budget may be misleading, there are some significant changes to the way retirees can claim their Social Security benefits in the future, and it may be in direct relation to the Social Security Trust Fund providing the $150 billion to the DI Trust Fund.

In order to keep checks and balances, reform to Social Security claiming loopholes needed to be closed. Section 831 of the law titled "Closure of Unintended Loopholes" details those specific changes.

The following pages will give an overview of what pre- and post- retirees need to be aware of.

Deemed Filing

The law provides incentives for delaying retirement benefits. Each year you defer your benefit beyond your Full Retirement Age (FRA) you receive an additional 8 percent increase in your monthly payment until age seventy.

In the past, this allowed for married couples to begin receiving spousal benefits while their own benefit continued to grow between age sixty-six and seventy.

Prior to the new law, if married individuals who were entitled to benefits as a worker who paid into the system, were also eligible as a spouse prior to their FRA, they had to apply for both benefits. This was called "deemed filing" because, when you apply for one of the benefits, you were "deemed" to also apply for the other simultaneously.

If you waited to file until FRA, you could then decide whether to file on your own working record or on your spouse's. It was possible to begin collecting a spousal benefit while allowing your personal worker benefit to earn the 8 percent delayed credit. Once you reached age seventy, it was possible to switch over from the spousal to your own personal (and increased) benefit.

The new law changes extend the deeming rules not only to individuals prior to their FRA but also now beyond their FRA. This means you can no longer collect one kind of benefit and then switch over to another—once you have filed, that's it, that's your benefit for the rest of your life, with the exception of the survivor's benefit if your spouse predeceases you.

Those who turned age sixty-two prior to December 31, 2015, will be grandfathered in under the old rules. Anyone under age sixty-two or turning sixty-two after December 31, 2015, will be subject to the new laws.

File and Suspend

Of all the Social Security claiming strategies, the file and suspend method seems to be the one people are most aware of, or, at the very least, they have heard about it to some extent.

Previous to law changes, an individual who reached their FRA (typically age sixty-six), could apply for retirement benefits. However, they could elect to immediately suspend the payments. This would allow their spouse to apply and receive spousal benefits.

In the meantime, the worker's benefits would earn delayed credits up to age seventy, where they would receive a higher income amount.

Under the new law, when you voluntarily suspend your benefit as in the example above, then all benefits payable on your record, including a spousal benefit, are suspended as well.

The law applies to those who request a voluntary suspension on May 1, 2016, and beyond, and you cannot request a suspension until you have reached your FRA.

Restricted Application

This new law also phases out the use of the restricted application strategy used by many dual-income earners.

Before, the strategy allowed couples to claim now and potentially claim more later, sometimes called the "double dip."

This is still available to those individuals born on or before January 1, 1954. You can execute the restricted application strategy in the following steps.

First, at FRA, the spouse with the higher earnings record applies for spousal benefits. This means the lower-earning spouse must already be receiving benefits on their own working record.

Next, the spouse with the higher earnings record switches to their own record at age seventy, effectively accruing the additional 8 percent per year increase on income from age sixty-six to seventy.

Here is an example:

Let's assume Ken & Barbie are both age sixty-six (with birthdays before the new deadline of 1/1/1954).

Ken's Social Security benefit on his own record is $2,000 per month.

Barbie's Social Security benefit on her own record is $1,100 per month.

Ken files a restricted application to receive *just* his spousal benefit and delay his individual benefit.

He receives $550 per month, or 50 percent of Barbie's benefit (which is the calculation for his entitled spousal benefit), from age sixty-six to seventy.

Barbie takes her benefit of $1,100.

When Ken turns age seventy, he then files an application for the benefit on his own record.

Ken now takes a benefit of $2,720 per month due to the compounding growth of the delay.

The advantage of using this strategy is Ken receives spousal benefits from age sixty-six to seventy, while his personal benefit continues to grow at 8 percent for four more years.

More importantly, if Ken were to pass away before Barbie, she would start receiving his higher, delayed amount as her survivor benefit.

In essence, his claiming decision will continue to be a benefit to his wife long after he is gone.

The following chart serves as a visual aid in understanding what changes have been made to which type of benefit recipient and any timeframes or deadlines associated with it.

Who Qualifies for Filing Strategies

BIRTH DATE	Currently Married		Unmarried Divorced Spouse		Surviving Spouse		Individual
	File & Suspend	*Restricted Application*	*File & Suspend*	*Restricted Application*	*File & Suspend or Restricted Application*		*File & Suspend or Restricted Application*
5/1/1950 or Earlier	Available at FRA—must have filed by 4/29/2016	Available at FRA (if otherwise eligible for spousal benefits)	Not Applicable	Still available at FRA as long as ex-spouse is older than 62	New rules not applicable. Can still independently choose timing of benefits.		Available at FRA—must have filed by 4/29/2016 for future reinstatement
1/1/1954 or Earlier	Not Eligible						No future lump sum reinstatement
1/2/1954 or After		Not Eligible		Not Eligible			

Where Do We Go From Here?

How do you know what to do in light of these recent changes?

The crucial thing to do, and the only thing we ask of everyone reading this book, is to take this seriously. There is no help for people who don't want help or won't take action.

A little bit of proactive action can make notable impacts on your current and financial future. We hope you found this section to be valuable, and we congratulate you on taking the vital first step in creating a solid retirement income financial plan. It all starts with finding the right information from the right people for you to be able to make the right decisions for you and your family.

APPENDIX 5

What You Need to Know About the New Tax Law

In the waning hours of 2017, President Donald Trump passed his long-promised tax reform in the United States.

A number of key changes to federal income tax rates were included in this reform, including:

- A reduction in the top federal income tax rate from 39.6 percent to 37 percent
- Doubling of the standard deduction
- Elimination of personal exemptions
- Elimination or reduction of many itemized deductions, such as:
    - Deduction for property taxes and/or state/local income taxes limited to $10,000
    - Deduction for alimony
    - Mortgage/home equity interest deduction

- Elimination of the "Pease Amendment" limitation on deductions, which means those who do continue to itemize can do so without limits.

In addition, the estate tax exemption was increased to just under $11.2 million (now $11.58 million in 2020) per taxpayer, with a 40 percent tax on transfers exceeding the amount of this exemption.

Likewise, the gift, estate, and generation-skipping tax exemptions increased, per individual, from $5 million to $10 million.

History of Estate Tax Exemptions

1980s	Estates Under $400K
1990s	Estates Under $600K
2000s	Estates Under $1.2M
2010	Estates Under $2.5M
2013	Estates Under $5.5M
2018	Estates Under $11.2M
2019	Estates Under $11.4M
2020	Estates Under $11.58M

While some of these new tax changes may be beneficial, it is crucial to remember virtually all of these provisions are only temporary—they are slated to sunset after the year 2025, reverting back to the previous level. Because of this, if you want to take advantage of these tax breaks, it is essential you do so now rather than later.

Your Next Steps: What Do You Do Now?

If you're totally comfortable with your knowledge of the financial landscape and the decisions you've made so far, you may be happy to act without professional advice.

But the complexity of today's financial environment and the pace of change means not many people have the time or expertise to confidently develop such a level of knowledge.

A financial advisor can help you gain more confidence with your retirement planning by helping you:

- Work out your financial goals and objectives.
- Clearly consider your current situation.
- Determine how to best manage your money.
- Create a budget, retirement plan, and an investing strategy.
- Create a plan to manage any debt you have.

The sheer importance of these decisions in your life means it can be very reassuring to have this support.

Keep in mind, financial advisors charge a fee—usually a percentage of your portfolio. However, this fee may be worth the assurance you receive when you lean on a qualified professional for help.

Advisors dealing with a wide variety of clients who have their own unique savings goals are widely available.

Here are some key points you might want to consider when searching for the right financial advisor:

Experience Working with People Like You

Financial advisors come in all shapes and sizes.

It can be worth it to find someone who has experience working with people in your income level and with your similar goals, assets, and liabilities.

Personal Chemistry

Look for an advisor you feel comfortable communicating with, and interview the advisor before you invest any money with them.

Expertise

Check their qualifications. You'd be surprised at how many people don't bother to check the credentials of a financial planner they're considering.

Independence

There's a clear conflict of interest when a financial planner works for a brokerage or fund he or she is required to steer you into.

Asks the Right Questions

Without a complete picture of current income, debt, assets, and liabilities, any plan drawn up won't help.

So, make sure they ask about your other investments, your tax return, and your debt situation (for example).

Tailors Advice to You

You want solutions tailored to your goals and needs rather than "cookie-cutter" or "one-size fits all" approaches.

Considers Estate Needs

Does he or she seem knowledgeable about estate planning and know how to minimize taxes while achieving your goals?

Good estate planning isn't just for millionaires. It is for everyone who wants to have control over his or her money.

Communicates Clearly

You should not be confused about your financial matters after talking with a prospective advisor.

You should understand everything he or she explains.

If You Prefer, Do It Yourself

If you're the type of person who likes to do things yourself, then start digging into the various options your investment company provides.

Let's say you started an IRA with your local bank. You will then be choosing from their investment options.

If you're looking at mutual funds, for example, they should provide you with the manager of the mutual fund and all of the businesses involved in said fund.

You can then research the success history of the fund manager and the companies.

If you're looking at stocks, find the company's website and research their track record.

If you're investing in your company's 401(k), the same holds true.

They should provide you with enough information about each investment option so you can then do some digging and research on your own.

If you're still confused, a number of online learning courses or books at the library break investments down to the basics.

You'll still want to research each company and investment option to make sure it's the right decision for you.

If you find the company isn't performing as you'd hoped, you can always modify your investments.

If what you've read here makes you want to learn more about your own retirement options, we'd be delighted to talk to you and discuss how we can help.

Please visit our website at www.retire-usa.com or call us at (732) 455-9990.

About Retirement Income Advisory Group

Financial planning is all about helping you address the "what-ifs" in life, and your retirement income is where we start the planning process.

Whether you are ten years away from retirement or ten years into retirement, we begin the planning process with a retirement income assessment.

We've found our clients enjoy the confidence of knowing where their next retirement paycheck will come from.

There's no such thing as a perfect investment, but we strive to create the right mix of strategies for your particular situation. These strategies help to streamline the process, remove the complication, and keep your goals and plans on track.

We consider it a privilege to provide a broad range of services to meet the varying needs of our clients.

We understand your goals and dreams can't be reached with a cookie-cutter approach. Thus, our services are uniquely tailored to address your specific concerns.

Our Mission

Our mission is to help keep clients from unknowingly and unnecessarily depleting their retirement savings and to create strategies designed to minimize the chances clients outlive their money.

About Denny Frasiolas

Denny Frasiolas is the managing partner and chief investment officer at Retirement Income Advisory Group, LLC, and he has been a financial professional since 2001.

He focuses on addressing clients' biggest concerns, with an emphasis on baby boomers, about wealth distribution planning and IRA/401(k) investment services. He's also an author, speaker, business consultant, and entrepreneur.

Denny knew he wanted a career in financial planning after he helped a family member who unexpectedly lost a loved one. He took responsibility to restore order and created a financial plan working to their benefit and helping them save more toward their nest egg.

When things suddenly change in life and there's no plan in place, you have to scramble to figure things out. Denny didn't want others to experience the same.

He holds a B.S. degree in finance and a B.S. degree in operations management from Indiana University's Kelley School of

Business, and he is also a licensed insurance professional. He received his master's degree in mathematics education from The College of New Jersey.

In addition, he has held several highly regarded positions in his professional career, including positions at Bank of America (formerly Fleet Bank), as a financial analyst, and at MetLife, as an investment advisor representative.

Denny has co-authored or contributed to three books with his colleague, Artie Bernaducci: **Strategies to Create Lifetime Income for Baby Boomers** (2016), **Financially Empowered, Taking Charge of Your Financial Life** (2018), and **The Baby Boomer Retirement Roadmap** (2020).

He is devoted to improving people's financial literacy and has spoken to the general public about retirement and financial income planning, Social Security, Medicare, and identify theft.

He's also been a guest at several corporations, speaking to insurance agency sales force personnel, attorneys, certified public accountants, financial advisors, and insurance agents.

Denny is also the co-founder of All Access Brokerage, LLC, which manages employee benefits and offers Medicare education and enrollment services for families in New York, New Jersey, and Pennsylvania.

He was a past chapter president of the 501(c)(3) nonprofit public benefit corporation The Society for Financial Awareness (SOFA.)

At the center of his life is his beautiful wife, Erin, as well as their three wonderful children, Parker, Mason, and Charlotte.

About Artie Bernaducci

Artie Bernaducci is the founder of Retirement Income Advisory Group, LLC, and he has been working in his favorite profession since 1991.

Throughout his career, his priority has been to help clients understand financial gobbledygook and help make it simpler for them to plan their retirement.

He quickly found effective ways to communicate so people could respond to sound advice and help improve their situation, instead of doing nothing about their future.

He has often stated, "It was no fun to try and help someone while I used language that caused their eyes to glaze over!"

After graduating from Ball State University in Indiana with a Bachelor of Science degree in soil science, he was unable to find work in his major area of study, so he went into the masonry business with his family and ran his own successful company for more than a decade.

The masonry business had its own gobbledygook, and, though it was a steep learning curve, Artie worked hard to simplify the language for day-to-day business.

With his transition to the financial world, it was a given he would apply this same approach and ensure clients could understand the industry "mumbo jumbo" in order to move forward with planning their retirement.

Artie is passionate about helping people and enjoys connecting with his clients. His focus includes retirement and financial income planning, and he especially enjoys assisting baby boomers who are approaching, or already in, retirement. He has also become a licensed insurance professional.

His aim is to educate clients and support them with the retirement knowledge they need to journey through their life stages.

He has co-authored the book ***Strategies to Create Lifetime Income for Baby Boomers*** with his colleague, Denny Frasiolas. He also speaks on retirement and financial income planning at many seminars.

Artie is married to his best friend and wife, Monica. He has four adult children, Rosaleen, Nicole, Jessica, and Louis, as well as four grandsons. Artie's main interests are family, bodybuilding, yoga, meditation, marketing, veganism, and "paying it forward."

Acknowledgments

We would like to thank writer Robert Greenshield whose contributions to this book, through research and rewrites, were invaluable. We would also like to thank editor Susan Wright for her deft hand and attention to detail, which propelled this project to the next level.

Thank you to Christopher Reyes, whose knowledge of Medicare and health care costs in retirement has helped our firm expand its ability to help clients in a much wider range of services. His passion for helping retirees navigate the maze of Medicare is exemplified in his contribution to this book.

www.ingramcontent.com/pod-product-compliance
Lightning Source LLC
Chambersburg PA
CBHW052355220526
45465CB00003BA/1114